How to use your Snap Revision Text Guide

This 'An Inspector Calls' Snap Revision Text Guide will help you get a top mark in your AQA English Literature exam. It is divided into two-page topics so that you can easily find help for the bits you find tricky. This book covers everything you will need to know for the exam:

Plot: what happens in the play?

Setting and Context: what periods, places, events and attitudes are relevant to understanding the play?

Characters: who are the main characters, how are they presented, and how do they change?

Themes: what ideas does the author explore in the play, and how are they shown?

The Exam: what kinds of question will come up in your exam, and how can you get top marks?

To help you get ready for your exam, each two-page topic includes:

Key Quotations to Learn
Short quotations to memorise that will allow you to analyse in the exam and boost your grade.

Summary
A recap of the most important points covered in the topic.

Sample Analysis
An example of the kind of analysis that the examiner will be looking for.

Quick Test
A quick-fire test to check you can remember the main points from the topic.

Exam Practice
A short writing task so you can practise applying what you've covered in the topic.

Glossary
A handy list of words you will find useful when revising 'An Inspector Calls' with easy-to-understand definitions.

AUTHOR: IAN KIRBY

ebook
To access the ebook, visit **collins.co.uk/ebooks** and follow the step-by-step instructions.

QR Codes
Found throughout the book, the QR codes can be scanned on your smartphone and link to a video working through the solution to the Exam Practice question on each topic.

ACKNOWLEDGEMENTS

The author and publisher are grateful to the copyright holders for permission to use quoted materials and images.

Every effort has been made to trace copyright holders and obtain their permission for the use of copyright material. The author and publisher will gladly receive information enabling them to rectify any error or omission in subsequent editions. All facts are correct at time of going to press.

Published by Collins
An imprint of HarperCollins*Publishers*
1 London Bridge Street
London SE1 9GF

HarperCollins*Publishers*
1st Floor, Watermarque Building, Ringsend Road, Dublin 4, Ireland

© HarperCollins*Publishers* Limited 2022

ISBN 9780008551506

First published 2022

10 9 8 7 6 5 4 3 2 1

British Library Cataloguing in Publication Data.

A CIP record of this book is available from the British Library.

Printed in the UK by Martins the Printer Ltd.

Commissioning Editors: Katherine Wilkinson and Clare Souza
Managing Editors: Craig Balfour
and Shelley Teasdale
Authors: Ian Kirby
Copyeditor: David Christie
Proofreaders: Jill Laidlaw and Fiona Watson
Typesetting: Mark Steward and QBS Learning
Cover designers: Kneath Associates and Sarah Duxbury
Production: Molly McNevin

MIX
Paper from
responsible source

FSC
www.fsc.org

FSC® C007454

This book is produced from independently certified FSC™ paper to ensure responsible forest management.

For more information visit:
www.harpercollins.co.uk/green

Contents

You must be able to: understand what happens at the start of the play.

The setting

The play is set in 1912, in the fictional industrial city of Brumley, North Midlands.

The opening stage directions reveal that the play takes place in the large suburban house of a wealthy businessman.

What is the situation?

The Birling family – Mr Arthur Birling, Mrs Sybil Birling and their two children, Eric and Sheila – have just finished dinner. There is a happy atmosphere.

The Birlings' guest is Gerald Croft, Sheila's wealthy fiancé, and they are all celebrating the couple's engagement.

Who are the characters?

The audience are briefly introduced to all the characters but the focus is on Arthur Birling.

After congratulating the young couple, he makes a speech about 1912's social and political climate.

He and Gerald are then left alone for a while and he talks of his social aspirations.

It is made clear that Gerald and the Birlings are pleased with their lives and see themselves as good people.

When Eric returns to the room, Mr Birling continues to talk to the young men about his experience of the world but is interrupted by the doorbell.

What changes the situation?

Inspector Goole arrives and the audience are told about the suicide of a young woman called Eva Smith.

Despite Mr Birling's status, the Inspector is confident, abrupt and mysterious.

Mr Birling sacked Eva from his factory two years ago, in September 1910. She led a group of young women to ask for a pay-rise of two-and-a-half shillings a week. This turned into an unsuccessful **strike**, after which the ringleaders, including Eva, were sacked.

Mr Birling finds himself defending his actions and Gerald supports him.

Hearing Eva's story, Eric feels sorry for her, which causes him to argue with his father.

The Inspector is clearly on Eva's side and this angers Mr Birling. He tries to intimidate the Inspector, which he ignores.

At this point, Sheila innocently enters the room.

Key Quotations to Learn

Arthur: 'It's one of the happiest nights of my life.'

Gerald: '[*laughs*] You seem to be a nice well-behaved family –'

Inspector: 'I'd like some information, if you don't mind, Mr Birling.'

Summary

- The Birlings are celebrating and they are very happy.
- The Inspector interrupts to discuss Eva Smith's suicide.
- Eva was sacked two years ago from Mr Birling's factory.
- The discussion of the suicide causes conflict on stage between Mr Birling, Eric and the Inspector.

Questions

QUICK TEST
1. Who are the four members of the Birling family?
2. What is the family celebrating?
3. Why does Inspector Goole arrive at the Birlings' house?
4. How is Eva Smith linked to Arthur Birling?
5. What different opinions do the characters have about Arthur's treatment of Eva?

EXAM PRACTICE
Using one or more of the 'Key Quotations to Learn', write a paragraph analysing how Priestley starts the play by establishing a happy, contented mood on stage.

Act 1 (part 2)

You must be able to: understand what happens in the second half of Act 1.

How does the focus shift to Sheila?

Sheila is upset by the news of the young woman's suicide and the Inspector reveals that the case involves more than just Mr Birling.

The Inspector gives some background to Eva's life and her situation. Sheila agrees with him that she led a pitiful life and needed **compassion**.

The Inspector tells of how Eva took a job at Millwards in December 1910 but she was then sacked in January 1911 after a complaint by a customer. Sheila recognises Eva's picture and runs out of the room upset.

When she returns, Sheila admits that it is her fault that Eva was sacked.

She explains that she was in a bad mood and felt Eva was laughing at her. She also admits she was jealous of Eva's prettiness. She is clearly upset but partly for herself rather than just about Eva's death.

How does the focus shift to Gerald?

When Sheila leaves the room upset, Mr Birling departs to speak to her and his wife.

Eric and Gerald are left with the Inspector. Eric gets angry and tries to leave the room but the Inspector insists that he stays.

After Sheila returns and confesses, the Inspector tells the three young people that Eva Smith changed her name to Daisy Renton. From Gerald's reaction, he is clearly disturbed by this news.

The Inspector and Eric go to the drawing room to speak to Mr and Mrs Birling, leaving Sheila and Gerald alone.

Sheila realises that Gerald was having an affair with Daisy during the previous spring/ summer of 1911.

Gerald thinks it can be hidden but Sheila realises that the Inspector knows everything already.

The Inspector returns to the dining room.

Key Quotations to Learn

Sheila: 'What do you mean by saying that? You talk as if we were responsible – '

Sheila: '[*miserably*] So I'm really responsible?'

Gerald: 'So – for God's sake – don't say anything to the Inspector.'

Summary

- Sheila feels sorry for Eva Smith.
- Sheila confesses that she complained about Eva and got her sacked from Milwards.
- Eva Smith changed her name to Daisy Renton.
- Gerald admits to Sheila that he had an affair with Daisy.

Questions

QUICK TEST
1. What does Sheila feel for Eva Smith when she first hears about her sacking and her suicide?
2. Why did Sheila get Eva sacked from Milwards?
3. What is significant about the reasons for Sheila being upset?
4. Who reacts strangely to the news that Eva changed her named to Daisy Renton?
5. What do we find out about Daisy's life during the spring/summer of 1911?

EXAM PRACTICE
Using one or more of the 'Key Quotations to Learn', write a paragraph analysing how Priestley presents the different reactions that Sheila and Gerald have to the Inspector.

Act 2 (part 1)

You must be able to: understand what happens in the first half of Act 2.

How is Mrs Birling presented?

Continuing the action from the end of Act 1, Gerald tries to get Sheila to leave so he can hide his involvement but she refuses.

As the Inspector talks about their joint responsibility, Mrs Birling enters very confidently. Sheila is instantly worried as she, Gerald and Arthur had all behaved the same way.

Mrs Birling behaves in a **superior** manner, referring to Eva's lower-class status, talking down to Sheila, acting grandly in front of the Inspector and referring to her husband's high status in the community. Despite this, the Inspector remains calm and blunt when speaking to her.

When Sheila reveals that Eric drinks too much, a fact that Gerald confirms, Mrs Birling is shocked and annoyed.

Sheila repeats her warning that her parents are making the situation worse and they are shocked to discover that Gerald knew Eva/Daisy.

How did Gerald know Daisy?

Gerald says he met Daisy in March 1911 in a bar. Sheila's parents don't want her to hear his story but she refuses to leave.

The reality of Daisy's death suddenly hits Gerald and he's visibly distressed.

He describes taking Daisy for a drink. She wanted to talk, having been upset by an encounter with Joe Meggarty (a city councillor who Gerald describes as a **womanising** drunk, which shocks Mrs Birling).

Gerald explains to the Inspector how Daisy had no money and was hungry. He innocently moved her into a friend's apartment and they later became lovers. Mrs Birling is disgusted by his behaviour.

Sheila points out that Gerald should be explaining to her not to the Inspector.

Gerald says that he didn't love Daisy but enjoyed being loved. He broke off the relationship in September 1911. The Inspector reveals that Daisy then went to the seaside; she wrote in her diary that she wanted to be alone to pretend her time with Gerald was continuing.

Gerald asks to go for a walk. Before he leaves, Sheila returns the engagement ring. She says she respects his honesty but they are now both different people.

Key Quotations to Learn

Inspector: '… we'll have to share our guilt.'

Mrs Birling: 'Girls of that class –'

Gerald: 'All she wanted was to talk – a little friendliness …'

Summary

- Gerald still hopes to hide his involvement with Eva/Daisy.
- The Inspector tells Gerald and Sheila that they are all responsible.
- Mrs Birling behaves in a superior way to the Inspector, Gerald and Sheila.
- Gerald reveals the details of his affair with Daisy, and Sheila breaks off the engagement.

Questions

QUICK TEST

1. Why does Gerald want Sheila to leave the room?
2. How does Mrs Birling criticise Eva Smith?
3. How does Mrs Birling behave in front of the Inspector?
4. Why is Sheila worried by her mother's behaviour?
5. What was Gerald's relationship with Daisy like?

EXAM PRACTICE

Using one or more of the 'Key Quotations to Learn', write a paragraph analysing how Priestley presents the different feelings that the characters have about Eva/Daisy.

Act 2 (part 2)

You must be able to: understand what happens in the second half of Act 2.

What was Mrs Birling's role in Eva Smith's death?

Mrs Birling says she doesn't recognise the photo of Eva. The Inspector and Sheila know she's lying.

The Inspector says that Mrs Birling is a prominent member of the Brumley Women's Charity Organisation and that Eva appealed to the charity two weeks ago.

Sybil reveals that Eva was using the name 'Mrs Birling', which she found insulting and so was instantly **prejudiced** against her.

Mrs Birling states that Eva only had herself to blame and says that it was her duty to use her influence to have the woman's claim refused.

The Inspector reveals that Eva was pregnant but clarifies that it wasn't Gerald's child.

Mrs Birling told the woman to look for the child's father as it was his responsibility. Sheila says her mother's behaviour was horrible, while Arthur suggests that it will look bad on them. In response, she points out that it was Arthur sacking Eva 'which probably began it all'.

How does the focus begin to turn on Eric?

At this point, it has not been made clear that Eric was the father of Eva Smith's child but the audience may be beginning to work it out. Just as Mrs Birling begins to be questioned, there is the sound of Eric leaving the house and the Inspector comments that he will be needed.

As the Inspector continues to question Mrs Birling, he pushes her into criticising the father of the **illegitimate** child. She also calls Eva a liar for claiming the man had offered her money but she thought it was stolen so didn't want to take it.

Mrs Birling refuses to accept any blame, saying it is the woman's fault first and the lover's second. She says the man should be made an example of and accepts that if the woman's story about stolen money is true then the lover is entirely to blame.

Sheila works out Eric's involvement and tries to stop her mother saying any more.

As Mr and Mrs Birling begin to realise the truth, Eric returns to the dining room.

Key Quotations to Learn

Mrs Birling: 'I'm very sorry. But I think she only had herself to blame.'

Mrs Birling: 'As if a girl of that sort would ever refuse money!'

Sheila: '[*with sudden alarm*] Mother – stop! – stop!'

Summary

- Eva was pregnant and asked Mrs Birling's charity for help.
- Mrs Birling didn't like the woman and used her influence to have the claim rejected.
- The Inspector manipulates Mrs Birling into stating that the father of Eva's child is entirely to blame for her death.
- The audience and the characters on stage gradually realise that Eric is the father.

Questions

QUICK TEST

1. What immediately turned Mrs Birling against Eva?
2. Does Mrs Birling regret rejecting Eva's claim for charity?
3. How do Sheila and Mr Birling respond differently to the news that Mrs Birling didn't help a pregnant woman who was asking for charity?
4. What did Mrs Birling think the woman was lying about?
5. Why does Sheila try to stop Mrs Birling from criticising the father of Eva's child?

EXAM PRACTICE

Using one or more of the 'Key Quotations to Learn', write a paragraph analysing how Priestley presents Mrs Birling's attitude towards Eva Smith.

Act 3 (part 1)

Video Solution · Exam Practice

You must be able to: understand what happens in the first half of Act 3.

How did Eric affect Eva Smith's life?

The story picks up from the end of Act 2 and Eric realises that everyone knows the truth.

The family argue over Eric's drinking and he retells how he met Eva in a bar.

After he turned aggressive, she let him into her flat where they had sex. At this point, Mr Birling orders Sheila to take her mother out of the room.

Eric continues his **confession**. He met Eva again, by accident, and they slept together. Eva revealed that she was pregnant but knew Eric didn't love her. To help her, he stole money from Arthur's office but she refused to take it.

How is Mr Birling presented at this point?

Arthur loses his temper several times before Eric's confession: first with the Inspector, who refuses to be intimidated by him, and then with Sheila when she doesn't want to leave the room.

He also shows his aggression during Eric's confession. When Eric points out that some of Birling's supposedly **respectable** friends have affairs, the Inspector has to stop Arthur from interrupting. He has another angry reaction when Eric admits to stealing.

Arthur also comes across badly when Eric explains his poor relationship with his father, feeling that he couldn't have asked him for help.

In addition to this, his reaction is still to cover the events up and avoid public scandal. It is particularly damning when he says he would give thousands of pounds to make the problem go away, showing his **capitalist** values rather than genuine regret.

How does the Inspector make his exit?

When Sheila and Sybil return, the Inspector tells Eric how Eva was rejected by his mother's committee, causing Eric to accuse Sybil of killing Eva and her own grandchild.

The Inspector sums up, telling them they all killed Eva Smith. He goes through the family, one by one, finally reminding Arthur that he destroyed a woman over two-and-a-half shillings.

The Inspector then focuses on the state of the country, pointing out that there are 'millions of Eva Smiths and John Smiths'. Talking to the Birlings (and the audience) he says, 'We are members of one body. We are responsible for each other.' He leaves with a warning that change will have to come.

Key Quotations to Learn

Arthur (to Sheila): '[*very sharply*] You heard what I said.'

Eric: '… you're not the kind of father a chap could go to when he's in trouble …'

Arthur (to Eric): '[*furious, intervening*] Why, you hysterical young fool – get back – or I'll – '

Inspector: 'We don't live alone. We are members of one body. We are responsible for each other.'

Summary

- Eric met Eva and made her pregnant.
- Eric accuses his mother of killing Eva and the baby, and says his father is unapproachable.
- The Inspector reminds the Birlings that they are all responsible for Eva Smith's death.
- The Inspector states his belief that all the members of society need to look after each other.

Questions

QUICK TEST
1. What negative aspects of Eric's character are revealed?
2. Why wouldn't Eva marry Eric?
3. What does Eric accuse his mother of?
4. In what way does Arthur not seem to have changed during the play?
5. What is the Inspector's final message before he leaves?

EXAM PRACTICE
Using one or more of the 'Key Quotations to Learn', write a paragraph analysing how Priestley presents Arthur Birling in the first half of Act 3.

Act 3 (part 2)

Video Solution — Exam Practice

You must be able to: understand what happens at the end of the play.

What happens after the Inspector leaves?

Arthur's reaction to the evening's events continues to be fear of the scandal. He also states his belief that he and Sybil can excuse their actions.

Sheila shows more guilt, pointing out that her parents haven't learned anything and criticising them for not focusing on the actual victim.

Sheila and Sybil begin to suspect that the Inspector wasn't a real police officer. Sheila doesn't think it matters because they still killed Eva Smith. However, Mr and Mrs Birling focus on the possibility of the whole affair remaining private if the police don't actually know.

How does Gerald's return alter things?

When Gerald returns, Arthur tries to stop Sheila from telling him about Eric and Sybil's involvement in Eva's death.

Gerald reveals that the Inspector wasn't a real police officer.

Mr and Mrs Birling are relieved and believe the secret can be kept amongst them. Arthur telephones the chief constable and it is confirmed that Inspector Goole doesn't exist.

While Gerald agrees with Arthur and Sybil, Sheila and Eric still feel guilt for what has happened.

Gerald, Arthur and Sybil begin to think the whole evening may have been a **hoax**. They ring the infirmary and find there is no dead woman.

How does the play end?

Arthur and Gerald relax and are pleased their bad experience is over. Arthur raises a toast to the family but Sheila and Eric refuse to take part.

Arthur feels that everything is back to normal. He laughs about the evening's events and suggests that Sheila asks Gerald for her engagement ring back. Gerald offers her the ring but she refuses.

Sheila and Eric realise that the others have learned nothing. She and Eric have been affected by the Inspector's words of warning as he left.

Arthur laughs at his two children as the phone rings. It is the police: a woman has died after swallowing disinfectant and an inspector is on his way.

Key Quotations to Learn

Sheila: 'Everything we said had happened really had happened.'

Arthur: '[*heartily*] Nonsense! You'll have a good laugh over it yet.'

Sheila: 'You began to learn something. And now you've stopped.'

Summary

- Gerald reveals that the Inspector wasn't a real police officer.
- They find out that there is no dead woman at the infirmary.
- Arthur, Sybil and Gerald relax, thinking everything can be covered up and forgotten.
- Sheila and Eric still feel guilty and cannot understand the others' behaviour.
- The play ends with a phone call from the police saying a woman has died and an inspector is on his way to the house.

Questions

QUICK TEST
1. What do Arthur and Sybil focus on after the Inspector leaves?
2. What do Sheila and Eric feel after the Inspector leaves?
3. How do Arthur, Sybil and Gerald feel when they realise that the Inspector wasn't real and that a woman hasn't died?
4. Why do Eric and Sheila feel differently to their parents?
5. How does the play end?

EXAM PRACTICE
Using one or more of the 'Key Quotations to Learn', write a paragraph analysing how Priestley presents the differences between Mr and Mrs Birling and their children.

Narrative Structure

You must be able to: explain the significance of the different ways Priestley has structured the play.

How does Priestley maintain the dramatic focus?

The play takes place on one evening, with each act opening immediately where the other left off.

The play takes place in one setting – the dining room of the Birlings' house.

The play has one central plot – the events leading to Eva Smith's death.

By taking this very singular approach, Priestley can focus on the drama and **tension** of the situation in order to emphasise his message about society.

To achieve this, the characters' involvements in Eva Smith's death are also dealt with one at a time. Characters not needed leave the stage, allowing Priestley to focus the audience on each person's responsibility.

How does Priestley raise and lower the tension?

To make the play and his social message memorable, Priestley uses the narrative structure to keep the **atmosphere** on stage tense and engaging.

Priestley starts each act by lowering the tension. A relaxed mood is established at the start of the play through the happy family meal, while the different character confessions at the beginning of Acts 2 and 3 lower the tension.

Different family arguments create brief spikes in tension, as does the way the Inspector comes into **conflict** with other characters.

At the end of the first two acts, Priestley raises the tension to a climax and includes a **cliffhanger**.

Act 1 ends with the unravelling of Sheila and Gerald's engagement, while the **climax** of Act 2 is even greater with Sybil and Arthur realising the truth about Eric.

Why does Priestley include the twist at the end?

When the Inspector leaves, the play seems to be over.

This trick by Priestley allows the audience to see whether the individual characters have learned anything or changed in any way. It also gives them time to judge each character's attitude to the social questions that Priestley has raised during the play through the character of the Inspector.

The play finally ends on a memorable cliffhanger, ensuring that the audience will question what they have seen and think more about the play's message.

Key Quotations to Learn

Sheila: 'And I hate to think how much he knows that we don't know yet. You'll see. You'll see.' (Act 1)

Arthur: '[*thunderstruck*] My God! But – look here – ' (Act 2)

'[*As they stare guiltily and dumbfounded, the curtain falls*]' (Act 3)

Summary

- Priestley uses a simple narrative structure (one plot, one set, one evening) in order to focus his social message.
- The drama is intensified by dealing with each character's guilt one by one, and removing them from the stage when they aren't needed.
- To make the play memorable, Priestley raises and lowers the tension throughout.
- Cliffhangers are used at the end of each act to keep the audience thinking about the events on stage.

Questions

QUICK TEST
1. In what way is the narrative structure of the play quite simple?
2. What narrative technique is used at the end of each act?
3. What things raise and lower the tension during the play?
4. What is Priestley trying to get the audience to focus on and think about?

EXAM PRACTICE
Using one or more of the 'Key Quotations to Learn', write a paragraph analysing how Priestley creates tension during the play.

You must be able to: understand the concept of class and the political ideas that are explored in the play.

What is meant by class?

This is a way of grouping different people in society according to their social status and how wealthy they are.

The most familiar labels are upper, middle and working class.

The upper class have the most money and status in society. This group of people are usually born into an old, established family that owns a lot of land and property, rather than gaining wealth through running a business. They often don't need to work. Upper-class families would often be linked to a title such as Lord, Sir or Duke. In the play, Gerald is upper class; his mother is Lady Croft, who Arthur refers to as coming from 'an old country family – landed people'.

The middle class are people who have recently earned a lot of money. They are usually well-educated with a good profession (such as doctors and lawyers) but can be anyone who has become wealthy through hard work. They are home-owners and aspire to having more money and social status. The Birlings are presented as a middle-class family, having made a lot of money through Arthur's business.

Some of the middle classes are disliked by the upper classes because they have the same amount of money but don't have the same 'breeding', meaning they aren't brought up to speak, behave and dress in the strict way that the upper classes see as respectable. This links to Arthur being aware that Lady Croft feels Gerald could have become engaged to someone 'better' than Sheila.

The working class are the poorest in society. They work for others, rather than being the bosses, and their wages are fairly low. They are linked to manual labour. The working class also includes the unemployed as they need to find work to get money, rather than being able to live off savings. Eva Smith is a good example of a working-class person: she had the job in Birling's factory but once she lost that job, she had no way to pay for food or rent.

What is capitalism?

Capitalism is a right-wing political belief in individual gain through hard work and a focus on profit. Capitalists accept that, for this to happen, there will always be people in society who are much better off than others.

Birling is a capitalist and talks happily about 'steadily increasing prosperity'. He disagrees with workers asking for more money and sacks Eva Smith and others for going on strike to try to achieve better wages.

What is socialism?

Socialism is a left-wing political belief in greater equality and fairness, especially for the poorest and most needy in society. Socialists believe working-class people should have more of a say in government and that wealth should be more evenly shared amongst the classes.

The Inspector represents socialist values, believing that people like Eva Smith should be better paid and, if they fall on difficult times, supported financially. He feels the poor are used or **exploited** in order to make the middle classes richer. When talking about the number of people in a similar position to Eva Smith, he adds, 'If there weren't, the factories and warehouses wouldn't know where to look for cheap labour. Ask your father.'

Summary

- Society can be divided into upper, middle and working class. In the play, these classes are represented by the Crofts, the Birlings and Eva Smith.
- The term capitalism refers to individual wealth through hard work. This links to Birling.
- Socialism refers to sharing wealth and looking after poorer people in society. This links to the Inspector.

Questions

QUICK TEST
1. In the play, which characters are linked to the upper class?
2. Which characters are middle class?
3. What class is Eva Smith?
4. Is Arthur Birling presented as a capitalist or a socialist? How can you tell?

EXAM PRACTICE
In Act 1, Arthur says to Gerald:
'I have an idea that your mother – Lady Croft – while she doesn't object to my girl – feels you might have done better for yourself socially – ... No Gerald, that's all right. Don't blame her. She comes from an old country family – landed people and so forth – and so it's only natural. But what I wanted to say is – there's a fair chance that I might find my way into the next Honours List. Just a knighthood, of course'.

Relating your ideas to the social context, write a paragraph explaining how Arthur is presented as having higher social aspirations and why he might want this.

J.B. Priestley and 1945

Video Solution   Exam Practice

You must be able to: understand how the play's meaning has been shaped by the author's life and the time in which he was writing.

Who was J.B. Priestley and how did his life affect his play?

John Boynton Priestley was born in 1894.

Although not as wealthy as the Birlings in his play, his was also a middle-class **suburban** family.

He left school at 16, took a job as a junior clerk, and began writing in his spare time.

He fought in the First World War (1914–1918) and spent many months in hospital after being badly injured. During the war, he would have fought side by side with all kinds of men regardless of their class.

After the war, Britain and many other countries were plunged into economic **depression**, with widespread poverty and a rise of political extremism. Priestley was influenced by his father's socialist views and wanted the world to become a more equal place.

By the 1930s, he was a successful writer. During the Second World War (1939–1945), Priestley was a radio broadcaster and his programme was very popular. He shared his socialist views and his hopes for a better Britain with listeners until the show was taken off air (because the government thought it too left-wing). These views appear throughout the play via the voice of the Inspector.

Priestley wrote *An Inspector Calls* in 1945. He continued his career as a playwright, novelist, essayist and political commentator until his death in 1984.

How does the time the play was written affect the play?

The two world wars were major contributors to the gradual erosion of Britain's strict class and gender divisions.

At war, men of different classes fought side by side despite any preconceived prejudices. At home, women kept the country running by taking on jobs they had not previously been encouraged to do.

By the 1920s, the Labour Party had grown out of different trade union and socialist movements to become the main opposition party to the Conservatives. The Labour Party had formed minority and coalition governments before and during the war but swept to power with a landslide victory in 1945.

It was this government that established the **welfare state**, introduced the National Health Service and promoted new housing estates where people of different classes would live side by side. However, the country could not change overnight and socialists saw that there was still a lot of work to do.

First performed in 1946, *An Inspector Calls* would have taken an audience back to 1912 and a very different Britain with very different values. It reminded them of the past in order to praise the present and keep pushing for further changes to achieve complete equality.

Summary

- J.B. Priestley grew up in the early 1900s and developed strong socialist beliefs.
- The two world wars began to change society by breaking down the rigid class system.
- The writing of the play coincided with the popularity of left-wing views in Britain.
- *An Inspector Calls* reminds its audience of a very different Britain.

Questions

QUICK TEST
1. How do Priestley's ideas appear through the character of the Inspector?
2. How might Priestley's wartime experiences have helped to shape his socialist principles?
3. How did the post-Second World War Labour government try to make Britain a more equal place?

EXAM PRACTICE
In Act 1, Arthur Birling says, 'We employers at last are coming together to see that our interests – and the interests of Capital – are properly protected. And we're in for a time of steadily increasing prosperity.'

Relating your ideas to the historical context, write a paragraph explaining how Birling's 1912 views might have seemed outdated when the play was first performed in 1946.

You must be able to: link the events of the play to its setting.

What were the Midlands like in 1912?

Although written in 1945, the play is set in 1912 (two years before the First World War).

The Midlands was a key area during the **Industrial Revolution** of the early nineteenth century. Towns and cities like Birmingham, Wolverhampton, Coventry and Nottingham became centres for industries such as textiles, coal mining and car manufacture.

The growth of factories meant the need for more workers. Many people had moved from small countryside villages to take the low wages on offer and live in cramped, unhygienic accommodation. The increase in low-skilled workers meant that more goods could be produced which, in turn, made the factory owners very rich.

Although conditions were improving, if people fell ill or were made unemployed, there was no benefits system to help so they would go hungry and become homeless.

Were men and women equal?

Attitudes towards gender were very different and women were considered to be 'the weaker sex'. Girls were brought up with the main aspirations of marriage and children.

Men dominated all aspects of life: home, workplace, church and government. This is often referred to as a patriarchy.

Men and women had specific roles and social expectations, and this actually became stricter the higher you moved up the class system.

Women in wealthy families were not expected to work. Instead, they looked after the home and took on charitable roles. Women in poorer families took unskilled jobs as domestic servants, shop assistants or factory workers. They were paid less than men and couldn't achieve the same level of promotion. Because of this, many women needed a man to support them so were easily seduced and used.

What political movements were important in 1912?

Trade unions had begun to form with the aim of securing better pay and conditions for workers. In 1912, a successful national strike secured a minimum wage for coal miners.

The Suffragettes were campaigning for gender equality, specifically trying to achieve the vote for women. They weren't successful until after the First World War.

The Labour Party was beginning to gain support.

What were the attitudes to morality in 1912?

Morality, having a clear sense of right and wrong, was central to society partly because the Christian Church was still a major influence.

The middle classes wanted to appear especially respectable because they aspired to higher status. However, as the Inspector suggests, their morality didn't often lead to them helping other people, just making judgements against them. There were huge double standards, with people appearing righteous and proper while actually behaving badly in secret.

Big towns and cities were full of temptations – such as sex, gambling and alcohol – so men often enjoyed themselves and hid it from their families (especially if they were married!). Sex outside of marriage was disapproved of, especially for a woman. Eric points out to his father that plenty of Arthur's apparently respectable friends get drunk and womanise.

Many women were unaware of this side of life because a respectable woman didn't hang around in bars or walk the streets after dark. Sybil is a good example of this: she doesn't like Sheila knowing slang like 'squiffy' and has no idea about Eric's real behaviour.

Summary

- Industrial areas had lots of poor workers and a few rich businessmen.
- Different groups were campaigning for class and gender equality.
- Despite the strong influence of the Christian Church on society, people (especially men) weren't always as moral as they seemed.

Questions

QUICK TEST
1. Why were people vulnerable if they fell ill or were unemployed?
2. What different areas of life and society did men take charge of?
3. In what ways were women unequal to men?

EXAM PRACTICE
Look at this conversation from Act 3 between Eric and Arthur:

Eric   I wasn't in love with her or anything – but I liked her – she was pretty and a good sport –

Arthur   [*harshly*] So you had to go to bed with her?

Eric   Well, I'm old enough to be married, aren't I, and I'm not married, and I hate these fat old tarts round the town – the ones I see some of your respectable friends with –

Arthur   [*angrily*] I don't want any of that talk from you –

Relating your ideas to the historical and social context, write a paragraph explaining how Priestley presents different attitudes to morality in this extract.

The Birlings' House

You must be able to: comment on how the staging of the play reveals things about the characters and themes.

How should stage directions be written about?

Remember that this is a play; you don't need to analyse the specific language of the stage directions. This is because stage directions are there to be performed not spoken aloud.

Instead, you should think about the effect of the stage directions. How do they affect the mood on stage? What do different things represent or **symbolise**? How do they show what characters are thinking and feeling?

How does J.B. Priestley describe the dining room set?

The dining room of a fairly large suburban house, belonging to a prosperous manufacturer. It has good solid furniture of the period. The general effect is substantial and heavily comfortable, but not cosy and homelike. [...]

The lighting should be pink and intimate until the Inspector arrives, and then it should be brighter and harder.

At rise of curtain, the four BIRLINGS and GERALD are seated at the table, with ARTHUR BIRLING at one end, his wife at the other. ERIC downstage, and SHEILA and GERALD seated upstage. EDNA, the parlour-maid, is just clearing the table, which has no cloth, of dessert plates and champagne glasses, etc., and then replacing them with decanter of port, cigar box and cigarettes. Port glasses are already on the table.

How does the setting reflect the family?

The set should show the audience that the Birlings have a high social status. This comes across through the size of the room and is also shown by the expensive furniture, with its sturdiness symbolising how confident the family are in their lives.

It is significant that all five characters are seated, which shows they are currently relaxed. In addition, it underlines their social superiority by contrasting with their maid, Edna, who is on her feet and clearing up after them.

However, the 'suburban' house (which indicates it is in a town or city rather than the countryside) shows the audience that this status is limited. They aren't upper class like the Crofts (which is why Arthur is so desperate for a status-changing knighthood).

Similarly, the general look of the stage shouldn't be warm and comfortable; this implies that there is something missing in this family: love.

How do the props reflect the family?

Different props reflect the family's wealth, in particular the champagne glasses. These are also useful to represent the difference between Arthur Birling and Eva Smith: while they show the Birlings' wealth, the champagne is also a stark contrast to the bleach that Eva drank to kill herself.

How is lighting used on stage?

Priestley is very specific about the lighting, which creates a rosy glow. This symbolises how the Birlings view themselves by making the audience think of the saying 'rose-tinted glasses', which refers to only seeing the best things in life. The Birlings are self-satisfied and ignore the immoral things that they do, partly because they don't see those things as wrong.

The entrance of the Inspector requires the lighting to change, with its increased brightness reflecting how the Birlings' lives are being examined and exposed. This altered lighting should help to create a mood of discomfort on stage.

Key Quotations to Learn

'substantial and heavily comfortable, but not cosy and homelike'

'pink and intimate ... brighter and harder'

'champagne glasses'

Summary

- The dining room set and its props reflect the Birlings' wealth and self-satisfaction. However, the set also reveals underlying problems in their lives.
- The set creates a visual contrast between the Birlings and the life of Eva Smith.
- The lighting emphasises how the Inspector shines a spotlight on their behaviour.

Questions

QUICK TEST
1. What features of the setting show the Birlings are wealthy?
2. What fault is pointed out about the appearance of the dining room?
3. How does the set establish that the characters are relaxed and happy?
4. When, how and why should the lighting alter?

EXAM PRACTICE
Using one or more of the 'Key Quotations to Learn', write a paragraph explaining how the set shows the Birlings' social superiority. Remember to focus on the effect that is created on stage and what this shows the audience.

Inspector Goole

You must be able to: analyse how Inspector Goole is presented in the play.

What does the Inspector represent?

The Inspector is described in his first stage directions as not needing physical size but projecting '[*an impression of massiveness, solidity and purposefulness*]'. This is to highlight that he brings with him symbolic powers of knowledge, morality and judgement.

He embodies the socialist viewpoint that members of society should care about each other. He is also a figure of morality and judgement.

Priestley uses the Inspector to expose one family's **hypocrisy** and their lack of morals and compassion. The change in lighting on stage when he enters ('[*brighter and harder*]') symbolises how he has come to reveal their secrets.

How is the Inspector presented as mysterious?

At the end of the play, we find out that there is no Inspector Goole at the local police station.

However, he is mysterious throughout the play. Like an **omniscient** narrator in a novel, he appears to know everything about the Birlings already. Sheila refers to this at the end of Act 1, '... he knows. Of course he knows.'

His behaviour also establishes mystery as he doesn't behave quite as the audience expect from a police inspector. He stares at characters before he speaks to them for the first time, refuses to let them see the photograph of Eva Smith until it is their turn and is clearly judgemental rather than **objective**.

Priestley's use of wordplay in Goole/ghoul suggests the character might not be a man but a higher power come to stand in judgement on the Birlings.

How does the Inspector create conflict and tension?

Priestley creates tension through the Inspector by having him ignore social **conventions**. Despite being of a lower class, he has all the power on stage. For example, he is not intimidated by Arthur or Gerald: '[*cutting through massively*]', '[*coolly, looking hard at him*]'.

He doesn't mind upsetting characters or challenging them, such as his effect on Sheila or his questioning of Sybil.

Priestley also uses the Inspector to turn the characters on each other. His presence creates arguments between the parents and their children, as well as ending Sheila and Gerald's engagement.

Key Quotations to Learn

'Yes, but you can't. It's too late. She's dead' (Act 1)

'Apologize for what – doing my duty?' (Act 2)

'... their lives, their hopes and fears, their suffering, and chance of happiness ...' (Act 3)

Summary

- Inspector Goole is a mysterious and powerful figure.
- He is not intimidated by the Birlings' superior class.
- He displays socialism and morality.
- He creates conflict and exposes the other characters on stage.

Sample Analysis

The Inspector is presented as powerful. When he challenges Mr and Mrs Birling, 'Don't stammer and yammer at me again, man ... *What did she say?*', the **imperative sentence** interrupts Arthur's attempt to stand up for Sybil, while the rhyming **colloquialisms** and the use of 'man', instead of the more respectful 'sir', belittle Arthur. This ignoring of social conventions shows the Inspector is confident and not intimidated by Arthur. His power can also be seen in his use of questioning. The italics indicate the actor should emphasise these words, showing his contempt for the family and that he won't let Mrs Birling evade his interrogation.

Questions

QUICK TEST

1. What socialist view does the Inspector represent?
2. How does he seem to go against social conventions?
3. What is unusual about his surname?
4. In what way does he expose the other characters?

EXAM PRACTICE

Using one or more of the 'Key Quotations to Learn', write a paragraph analysing how Priestley presents the Inspector as a figure of morality.

Arthur Birling

You must be able to: analyse how Arthur Birling is presented in the play.

How is Birling presented as self-satisfied?

At the start of the play, Birling shows off his wealth and experience.

He boasts about the quality of his port and cigars, and praises his own qualities (twice repeating the phrase 'hard-headed business man').

His values of selfishness and survival of the fittest are shown in his words to Eric and Gerald: 'a man has to make his own way – has to look after himself'.

How does Priestley show Birling is the head of the house?

Arthur Birling is a **patriarch**. He is placed symbolically at *'one end'* of the table to show his importance.

He gives orders, such as telling Sybil to praise the cook. Significantly, the cook isn't named (he may not know or care) and he presumably considers it below himself to speak to her personally. This shows his attitude to the working class, as well as to women and their roles.

Birling interrupts other characters and makes long speeches. Priestley gives him the most lines in the opening of the play to demonstrate his dominance.

Because he expects to be respected, he is regularly angered by the way the Inspector interrupts or ignores him.

How are Birling's aspirations revealed?

Birling has gained lots of money but not the social status he wants. His *'provincial'* accent shows he isn't upper class but his hope for a knighthood reveals he wants to be.

His lack of natural class is a personal grievance, acknowledging that Gerald's mother thinks the Birlings are socially **inferior**.

He is happy for Sheila's engagement, partly due to the status it gives him through the Croft name: 'Crofts Limited are both older and bigger than Birling and Company – and now you've brought us together'.

How can the audience tell that Birling isn't as wise as he thinks?

Although written in 1945, the play is set in 1912, which allows Birling to be wrong in his confident speeches about the future.

This is **dramatic irony** and is most obvious in his lines about war ('And I say there isn't a chance of war') and the *Titanic* ('unsinkable, absolutely unsinkable'). Techniques such as short sentences and repetition are used to emphasise his errors. Priestley also uses the *Titanic* to **foreshadow** the sinking of the Birlings: the ship's unsinkable luxury mirrors the family's self-assured, wealthy appearance.

Key Quotations to Learn

'... working together – for lower costs and higher prices ...' (Act 1)

'You've a lot to learn yet. And I'm talking as a hard-headed, practical man of business.' (Act 1)

'And we don't guess – we've had experience – and we *know*.' (Act 1)

Summary

- Arthur Birling is a dominant, patriarchal figure.
- He is wealthy and pleased with himself but wishes for greater social status.
- He believes he has wisdom and experience but Priestley uses dramatic irony to undermine this.

Sample Analysis

Birling is presented as dominant through the way he controls conversations, 'Now you three young people, just listen to this –, making him come across as a **traditional** patriarch. The imperative sentence indicates he is in charge, which is emphasised by the discourse marker 'Now' and his use of the second person to demand their attention. On stage this can also be shown by the **dramatic pause** before he continues his speech. Birling's use of the **patronising** adjective 'young' also suggests he is trying to enhance his sense of experience and wisdom.

Questions

QUICK TEST

1. Why does Priestley give Birling the greatest number of lines and have him interrupt and give orders?
2. What phrase does he repeat to show his self-confidence?
3. As well as his love for his daughter, why is he pleased about her engagement to Gerald?
4. Why is Birling's confident belief that there will be no war important?

EXAM PRACTICE
Using one or more of the 'Key Quotations to Learn', write a paragraph analysing how Priestley presents Arthur Birling as a confident man.

You **must be able to:** analyse how Mrs Birling is presented in the play.

What kind of woman is Sybil?

Sybil is presented as a traditional early-twentieth-century middle-class woman, focused on the household and her children. Although she is his social superior, and sometimes tells him off for a lack of correct **etiquette**, she usually defers to her husband and follows his lead. She is told to pass on a message to the cook, accepts that men 'spend nearly all their time and energy on their business', leaves the room with Sheila so the men can talk together and looks to Arthur to take charge.

How is Sybil presented as feeling superior?

When she meets the Inspector, she thinks she is above him and speaks '[*haughtily*]' and '[*rather grandly*]'. She is surprised by his lack of respect, 'That – I consider – is a trifle impertinent, Inspector.'

To assert herself, she refers to her husband's social position.

She suggests she is better than other characters, taking a moralistic view of Gerald's affair when calling it 'disgusting' and boasting that she was the 'only one of you who didn't give in' to the Inspector in Act 3.

How does Priestley show her hypocrisy?

Sybil presents herself as moralistic, with a prominent role in the Brumley Women's Charity Organisation. She talks about helping others and doing her duty.

However, she turned down Eva's application for support, looking down on her for being single and pregnant. She refers to 'a girl of that sort', showing her dislike of the lower classes and what she sees as Eva's lack of sexual decency.

Throughout the play, she refuses to accept any blame and excuses herself by repeating the word '**justified**'.

She criticises Eva's lover's lack of morals but these turn out to be the qualities of her own son.

How is Sybil presented as a bad mother?

Sybil does not really know her children, particularly Eric. She doesn't realise he has a drinking problem and cannot believe he could ever have an affair. He subsequently accuses her of having killed her own grandchild and tells her she never tried to understand him.

Mr Birling calls Eric 'spoiled' and this reflects on Sybil's parenting skills.

She also belittles her children, not wanting them to grow up or develop their own views: 'He's only a boy', 'It would be much better if Sheila didn't listen to this story at all.'

Key Quotations to Learn

'Girls of that class – ' (Act 2)

'I'm very sorry. But I think she only had herself to blame.' (Act 2)

'Besides, you're not that type – you don't get drunk – ' (Act 3)

Summary

- Mrs Birling displays a traditional female role in the house.
- She sees herself as superior to people of the lower classes.
- She presents herself as moral and charitable.
- She is revealed to be a hypocrite and a bad mother.

Sample Analysis

Sybil's lack of social responsibility is shown throughout the play by her refusal to accept any blame for what happened to Eva Smith, 'So I was perfectly justified in advising my committee not to allow her claim'. She repeats the adjective 'justified' several times in Act 2 to excuse her actions and this stubborn, selfish attitude is emphasised here by the **adverb** 'perfectly'. She shows off her social power by linking the committee to the possessive **pronoun** 'my' and using the verb 'allow', reminding the audience of how she could have helped if she had wanted to.

Questions

QUICK TEST
1. In what ways does Sybil conform to the gender expectations of the time?
2. Why does she feel superior to others?
3. What does her charity role show about her?
4. What is her relationship with Eric like?

EXAM PRACTICE
Using one or more of the 'Key Quotations to Learn', write a paragraph analysing how Priestley presents Sybil's attitudes to others.

Sheila Birling

You must be able to: analyse how Sheila is presented in the play.

What is Sheila's life like?

The opening stage direction says that Sheila should be presented as '[*very pleased with life and rather excited*]'.

She is in her 20s and has an easy life. Following the traditional social expectations for the daughter of a wealthy family in the early twentieth century, Sheila doesn't work. She is obedient to her parents and engaged to marry Gerald.

She still refers to her parents as 'Mummy' and 'Daddy', suggesting her class and also her childishness.

What does her treatment of Eva Smith show about her?

She has Eva sacked because she felt she was mocking her. Sheila admits she over-reacted because she was in a bad mood and was jealous that Eva was prettier than her.

She uses her social power, as a good customer who is about to marry a wealthy man, to have a lower-class woman punished.

How does Sheila respond to Eva Smith's actions?

When she first hears of Eva Smith's death, she is sympathetic but more focused on how it's made her feel sad: 'I've been so happy tonight. Oh I wish you hadn't told me.'

This self-centred response continues when she realises she had Eva sacked from Milwards: 'I feel now I can never go there again'.

These responses reflect the selfish values that she has been brought up with.

However, in Act 2, she begins to reflect more on her responsibility: 'And I know I'm to blame – and I'm desperately sorry – but I can't believe – I won't believe – it's simply my fault that in the end she – she committed suicide.' Her guilt is still **juxtaposed** with a refusal to take ultimate responsibility but the use of dashes indicates that her speech should sound uncertain, as if she is struggling with her **conscience**.

How is Sheila presented as more insightful than her family?

Whereas Arthur, Sybil and Gerald deny their responsibility and try to cover up their involvement, Sheila quickly realises that they cannot hide the truth.

At the end of Act 2, she contributes to the increasing tension by trying to stop her mother from incriminating herself and Eric (having already worked out that he fathered Eva's child).

Key Quotations to Learn

'... I'll never, never do it again to anybody.' (Act 1)

'No, he's giving us the rope – so that we'll hang ourselves.' (Act 2)

'Mother – I begged you and begged you to stop –' (Act 2)

Summary

- Sheila has an easy happy life and a high social status.
- She used her status to have Eva sacked.
- She shows some guilt for what happened but is also busy feeling sorry for herself.
- Unlike the rest of the family, she realises that the Inspector already knows the full story.

Sample Analysis

Sheila realises the family's position long before the others. When she tries to warn her mother, '[*urgently, cutting in*] Mother, don't – please don't. For your own sake, as well as ours', Sheila's tone of voice creates tension on stage, which is highlighted by the repetition of the imperative 'don't'. Interrupting and calling Sybil 'Mother' instead of the previous 'Mummy' also creates a more serious mood. The second sentence shows that she senses the family are in danger but reminds the audience that, despite feeling some guilt about Eva, she is still focused on her own wellbeing.

Questions

QUICK TEST

1. Why does Sheila have social status?
2. What feelings cause her to have Eva sacked?
3. How does Sheila begin to change?
4. What does she realise about Eric, long before the rest of the family?

EXAM PRACTICE

Using one or more of the 'Key Quotations to Learn', write a paragraph analysing how Priestley presents Sheila's response to the Inspector's investigation.

Eric Birling

Video Solution   Exam Practice

You must be able to: analyse how Eric is presented in the play.

What first impressions are the audience given of Eric?

At the start of the play, Eric seems an outsider. He is the last character to speak and is absent from the second act.

The opening stage direction describes him as '[*not quite at ease*]' and this is evident throughout Act 1, such as when he stops himself mid-sentence during a discussion about women and his reaction to Gerald's joke about misbehaviour.

He first gains the audience's attention when he bursts out laughing for no reason. This, and his squabble with Sheila, makes him seem immature. Mr and Mrs Birling regularly talk down to him, for example, calling him a 'Silly boy!', despite him being in his twenties.

Priestley draws attention to his drinking through the stage directions , '[*Takes decanter and helps himself*]', and this becomes more important later on.

How does he feel about what he has done?

Unlike the others, Eric makes no attempt to excuse his behaviour.

The stage directions repeatedly point out that he should speak '[*miserably*]'. He is clearly ashamed of his actions and this helps to explain his strange and distant behaviour at the start of the play.

How does Eric clash with his parents?

Early on, he displays different values to his father. He suggests that Eva was right to go on strike and receives an angry response from Arthur.

When Eric returns in Act 3, the family have been discussing his behaviour and, especially Sybil, making the situation worse for him. Instead of supporting him, his parents are angry about the impending scandal. When he asks for a drink, his father refuses '[*explosively*]' but the Inspector intervenes, saying 'look at him. He needs a drink now just to see him through.'

He later tells his father that he's never been able to talk to him and he says a similar thing to his mother: 'You don't understand anything. You never did. You never even tried – you – '.

When he finds out that his mother turned Eva away from the charity, he accuses her of killing her own grandchild.

After the Inspector has left, Mr Birling singles Eric out as the person to blame.

Key Quotations to Learn

'Why shouldn't they try for higher wages?' (Act 1)

'... I hate these fat old tarts round the town – the ones I see some of your respectable friends with – ' (Act 3)

'... you killed them both – damn you, damn you – ' (Act 3)

Summary

- Eric acts strangely at the start of the play.
- His behaviour is explained when it is revealed that he made Eva pregnant.
- The play gradually builds up the fact that he has a drink problem.
- He clashes with his parents and this reaches a climax just before the Inspector leaves.

Sample Analysis

Eric's shame is clear when he describes his first night with Eva, 'And I didn't even remember – that's the hellish thing. Oh – my God! – how stupid it all is!', using the adverb 'even' to emphasise his self-reproach for his drunken behaviour. This can also be seen in the contrasting religious language, implying **sin** and confession. Priestley's use of repeated exclamations, punctuated by dramatic pauses, shows the distress that should be apparent in his voice on stage.

Questions

QUICK TEST
1. Why does Eric seem different to the other characters at the start of the play?
2. How does he disagree with his father about the factory workers?
3. How does he feel about his behaviour?
4. What does he feel about his relationship with his parents?

EXAM PRACTICE
Using one or more of the 'Key Quotations to Learn', write a paragraph analysing how Priestley presents Eric's conflict with his parents.

You must be able to: analyse how Gerald is presented in the play.

What is Gerald's relationship with Arthur like?

Gerald has a fairly equal relationship with Arthur. This is mainly because he is of a higher class, being the son of Sir George and Lady Croft, so Arthur respects him and hopes to gain status through him.

Like Arthur, Gerald is a businessman. When Eric argues with his father about the factory strike, Gerald sides with Arthur's viewpoint: 'I should say so!'

Although Birling lectures Gerald, he also confides in him about the possibility of his knighthood. It is clear that Mr and Mrs Birling like and trust their future son-in-law.

How does Priestley present Gerald's relationship with Eva Smith?

Gerald knew Eva as Daisy Renton. He initially denies it but Sheila sees through his lies. He plans to keep it a secret from the Inspector but Sheila says he won't be able to.

When he met Daisy, he found her attractive and felt sorry for her so he gave her money and a place to stay. He just wanted to help her but she became his mistress as well: 'I suppose it was inevitable. She was young and pretty and warm-hearted – and intensely grateful.' The dash creates a pause to suggest Gerald realises that Eva may have felt obliged because he was her only support.

He admits that she loved him more than he loved her and he eventually broke off the relationship. He is distressed when he thinks about her death.

How do the other characters' opinions of him change?

In contrast to their happiness at the start, once Sheila works out about the affair she loses respect for Gerald: 'Oh don't be stupid. We haven't much time.' As he tells his story, she mocks him, 'You were the wonderful Fairy Prince. You must have adored it, Gerald.'

After his confession, Sheila says she believes his intentions were initially good but she can no longer be his fiancée: 'You and I aren't the same people who sat down to dinner here.'

Sybil calls his story a 'disgusting affair', which contrasts with the start of the play when she stops Sheila from teasing Gerald for having worked so much over the summer (when he was actually with Daisy).

Perhaps for selfish reasons, Arthur doesn't particularly change his opinion of Gerald. When Sheila breaks off the engagement, he tries to reason with her, 'Now, Sheila, I'm not defending him. But you must understand that a lot of young men – '.

Key Quotations to Learn

'... we're respectable citizens and not criminals.' (Act 1)

'We can keep it from him.' (Act 1)

'She didn't blame me at all. I wish to God she had now.' (Act 2)

Summary

- The Birlings are happy to have Gerald as Sheila's fiancé.
- He tries to hide his relationship with Eva/Daisy from Sheila and the Inspector.
- Gerald wanted to help Eva/Daisy but it turned into an affair.
- He is upset by the news of Eva's death and understands when Sheila breaks off the engagement.

Sample Analysis

Priestley makes it clear that Gerald is upset by Eva Smith's death, '[*distressed*] Sorry – I – well, I've suddenly realised – taken it in properly – that she's dead – ', and the specified tone of voice makes his feelings clear on stage. His stumbling speech also shows a feeling of shock. He repeats 'I' and rephrases what he is trying to say, with the dashes creating pauses that demonstrate how he is almost lost for words. This is emphasised by the way his speech is left unfinished to show he is having trouble continuing.

Questions

QUICK TEST

1. In what ways does Gerald pretend to be something that he's not?
2. Why does Arthur like Gerald?
3. What were the honourable aspects of his part in Eva Smith's life?
4. What were the dishonourable aspects of his part in Eva Smith's life?

EXAM PRACTICE

Using one or more of the 'Key Quotations to Learn', write a paragraph analysing how Priestley presents Gerald's public image as a lie.

Eva Smith and Edna

You must be able to: analyse how Eva Smith and Edna are presented in the play.

How does Priestley present Eva Smith?

Eva Smith never appears on stage; instead, the audience are given details about her by the other characters. This is important because it symbolises how the working classes play a large role in the Birlings' life and wealth but they are almost invisible.

The Inspector explains that she has committed suicide by drinking disinfectant. He later reveals that she was pregnant.

Arthur describes her as lively and hard-working. Like Gerald and Sheila, he also comments on her good looks.

She is presented as moral (she won't take Eric's stolen money) and having a strong belief in fairness and equality (organising the strike at the factory). It is significant that she comes across as having better values than the people who ruined her life.

Eva also used the name Daisy Renton.

What is Eva Smith being used to represent?

Eva is used by Priestley as an 'every-woman' and he draws attention to this by giving her the common surname 'Smith'.

She represents the working classes: both their financial struggles and the prejudice against them from those of a higher status.

She also shows the audience some of the obstacles that women faced in society:

- The **dominance** of men (Arthur is her employer, Eric forces his way into her lodgings).
- Being treated like a sexual object (Joe Meggarty's advances, Eric only wanting her for sex).
- The difficulty in being independent or self-sufficient (she is unemployed and hungry when she meets Gerald and she is dependent on his support).
- Prejudice about sexual activity (Sybil is prejudiced against her partly because she is pregnant but unmarried).

What is the significance of Edna?

Although she is not on stage a great deal, Edna is another representation of the working classes. She is a servant, cleaning away the table and fetching drinks.

The Birlings mostly ignore her but Arthur and Sybil acknowledge her presence in relation to the jobs they want doing.

She is addressed informally as 'Edna' but she responds to her employers as 'ma'am' or 'sir', showing the differences in status between the classes.

Key Quotations to Learn

Inspector: 'There are a lot of young women living that sort of existence in every city and big town in this country ...' (Act 1)

Inspector: 'She was here alone, friendless, almost penniless, desperate.' (Act 2)

Inspector: 'Just used her ... as if she was an animal, a thing, not a person' (Act 3)

Summary

- Eva is only described by others, never seen.
- She has committed suicide.
- She represents the plight of working-class women.
- She is shown to have better values than the seemingly more respectable Birlings.

Eva Smith's Timeline

Sep 1910	After helping to organise a strike over wages at Birling and Company, Eva is sacked.
Dec 1910	She gets a job at Milwards.
Jan 1911	Sheila complains about Eva and she is sacked.
March 1911	Eva, who has now changed her name to Daisy Renton, meets Gerald. He finds her a place to live and she becomes his lover.
Sep 1911	Gerald breaks off his relationship with Daisy. She goes to live by the seaside for two months.
Nov 1911	Eva meets Eric. They become lovers and she gets pregnant. After she realises that Eric is supporting her with stolen money, she leaves him.
Spring 1912	Eva, using the name Mrs Birling, asks for help from the Brumley Women's Charity Organisation but it is refused.
Spring 1912	Two weeks later, Eva Smith commits suicide.

Questions

QUICK TEST

1. Which two sections of society does Eva Smith represent?
2. In what different ways is she treated badly by characters in the play?
3. In what ways does she appear to have better values than the Birlings?
4. What does Edna show about the Birlings' attitude to the working class?

EXAM PRACTICE

Using one or more of the 'Key Quotations to Learn', write a paragraph analysing how Priestley uses Eva Smith to present the need for society to be more caring.

You must be able to: analyse how the characters change during the play.

Arthur and Sybil Birling

Mr and Mrs Birling change the least in the play. Their treatment of Eva Smith is exposed and their relationship with their children is damaged. The audience see their confidence and status weakened. However, once the Inspector leaves and they decide it was all a hoax, they go back to their old, self-centred ways. Arthur even makes a joke about the evening: '[Imitating Inspector in his final speech] You all helped to kill her. [Pointing at Sheila and Eric, and laughing]'.

Gerald

Like Arthur and Sybil, once Gerald decides it is a hoax, he cheers up and tries to get Sheila to wear the engagement ring again. The audience are shown his disregard for the working classes when he says, 'What girl? There were probably four or five different girls.' He does not mind how many lives have been ruined so long as it isn't going to be a public scandal.

Sheila and Eric

The Birling children are most affected by the events of the play. Priestley does this to reflect society's changing values between the young and the old, suggesting that the young represent hope for a more equal, compassionate future.

Sheila's distress and regret can be seen as early as Act 1 although it is often focused on her feeling sorry for herself.

By the end of the play, Sheila feels genuine remorse and she realises that it doesn't matter if the Inspector was real or not, 'I tell you – whoever that Inspector was, it was anything but a joke.'

She wants her family to change their ways and Priestley has her repeat the Inspector's words, 'Fire and blood and anguish', to show that she understands his revolutionary warning.

Eric is similarly altered and describes himself as frightened by the Inspector's final words.

Priestley focuses on Eric's broken relationship with his parents: '[quietly, bitterly] I don't give a damn now whether I stay here or not.'

Key Quotations to Learn

Arthur: '... there'll be a public scandal – unless we're lucky – and who here will suffer from that more than I will?'

Sheila: '... you don't seem to have learnt anything.' (Act 3)

Eric: 'You're beginning to pretend now that nothing's really happened at all.'

Mrs Birling: 'In the morning they'll be as amused as we are.'

Gerald: 'Everything's alright now, Sheila.'

Summary

- Arthur, Sybil, and Gerald do not really change. Although disturbed by the night's events, once they decide it's a hoax, they return to normal.
- Sheila and Eric are upset and regret their actions. They can't understand their parents' attitudes and begin to see they must all change their behaviour.

Sample Analysis

By the end of the play, Arthur's social attitudes have not changed. In Act 1, he believes that the working classes need to be kept in their place, 'If you don't come down sharply on some of these people', with the adverb suggesting harshness and a lack of compassion while the **noun phrase** 'these people' reminds us that he sees the workers as all the same rather than individuals to be cared for. This outlook is still held at the end of the play, 'Probably a Socialist or some sort of crank', and Priestley has Birling disparagingly link socialism to a colloquial term for a madman or eccentric: he still sees it as unnecessary, even ridiculous, to care for people who are less fortunate.

Questions

QUICK TEST
1. What is Arthur most worried about once the Inspector has left?
2. In what way do Eric and Sheila's attitudes at the end of the play differ to those of their parents?
3. What does Gerald ask Sheila that shows he thinks nothing has changed?
4. What has changed between Eric and his parents?

EXAM PRACTICE
Using one of the 'Key Quotations to Learn', and another from elsewhere in the play, analyse how Priestley shows a character changing or staying the same.

Morality

You must be able to: analyse how the theme of morality is presented in the play.

What is morality?

Morality is a sense of right and wrong. It is often linked to religion but Priestley explores it in terms of society, considering personal behaviour and the treatment of others.

Which characters see themselves as 'moral'?

Gerald and the Birlings base their sense of morality on their class. Because they have status they assume they are superior. Priestley challenges this view in Act 1:

Gerald: ... we're respectful citizens and not criminals.

Inspector: Sometimes there isn't as much difference as you think.

Sybil presumes moral superiority when she feels her charity work gives her the right to judge others. When she is called a 'prominent' member of the charity, Priestley is suggesting the role is more about making herself look good in society.

How does Priestley use the seven deadly sins?

Priestley draws on Christian ideas to shows his characters' lack of social morality.

When the play begins, the audience see the sin of *gluttony* (eating and drinking wastefully or to excess). The table is being cleared of '[*dessert plates and champagne glasses, etc.*]' and everyone is drinking port. Priestley uses this scene to contrast, in Act 2, with Gerald describing Eva as being hungry. Eric, through his drinking, becomes the particular focus of this sin.

Arthur is guilty of *greed* through his desire for more money and status. When he describes his 'duty to keep labour costs down', Priestley uses the **noun** 'duty' ironically to show Birling's lack of moral understanding.

Birling is also full of *wrath* or anger throughout the play, sacking Eva partly out of anger and losing his temper with the Inspector and his children.

Sheila represents *envy* – she has Eva sacked partly out of jealousy over her prettiness. This links to wrath, as she admits to being in a bad mood, while her lifestyle suggests *sloth* or laziness. Sloth also relates to the other characters' social laziness as they are unwilling to support people in need.

Sybil's *pride* is obvious in the way she speaks, regularly emphasising her status, such as the stress on the personal pronoun in the line, *'I'm* talking to the Inspector now'.

Gerald and Eric display *lust* when each makes Eva their mistress and loves her less than she loves them. This sin is extended to Joe Meggarty and Arthur's friends to criticise their attitudes to women.

Key Quotations to Learn

Inspector: '... you might be said to have been jealous of her.' (Act 1)

Sybil: '... she called herself Mrs Birling ... a piece of gross impertinence ...' (Act 2)

Eric: 'I wasn't in love with her or anything ...' (Act 3)

Summary

- The characters consider themselves to be moral because of their social status.
- They lack social morality and compassion for the people around them.
- Priestley links the Birlings and Gerald to the seven deadly sins.

Sample Analysis

Priestley presents a lack of morality amongst Brumley's middle classes. When Gerald reveals that a town councillor, Joe Meggarty, is 'a notorious womanizer as well as being one of the worst sots and rogues', Priestley links him to the sins of lust and gluttony, using the **superlative** 'worst' to emphasise his poor values. By using the **adjective** 'notorious', it is also clear that lots of people know about Meggarty's behaviour and yet he still holds a position of responsibility. Priestley is criticising the higher classes' abuse of power and how they ignore in themselves what they would condemn in people of lower status.

Questions

QUICK TEST
1. How is Arthur linked to the sin of greed?
2. How is Eric linked to lust and gluttony?
3. What was Sheila envious of?
4. Where is Sybil shown to consider herself as morally superior to others?

EXAM PRACTICE
Using one or more of the 'Key Quotations to Learn', write a paragraph analysing how Priestley presents the characters as lacking morality.

Survival of the Fittest

You must be able to: analyse how the theme of survival is presented in the play.

What is survival of the fittest?

This term was first used in the late 1800s to describe how, in the animal kingdom, weak species die out and the strongest survive. In a capitalist society, people with power and money will usually do better than those without. The term is sometimes used by capitalists to justify selfish economic behaviour (such as very low wages or trying to put others out of business).

What is Arthur's view?

Arthur promotes the idea of survival of the fittest to Eric and Gerald, telling them that a man 'has to look after himself ... so long as he does that he won't come to much harm.'

His words are selfish and, near the end of the play, Eric mocks how these words returned to haunt his father: '[*laughs bitterly*] I didn't notice you told him that it's every man for himself.'

What does the Inspector think?

It is symbolic that, when he gives his selfish speech to Eric and Gerald, Arthur is interrupted by the Inspector's arrival: '[*We hear the sharp ring of a front door bell. Birling stops to listen*]'.

Part of the Inspector's role is to challenge Arthur's view of the survival of the fittest. He can be seen as representing Priestley's socialist views.

When Arthur explains his refusal to pay his workers more, the Inspector says 'Why?' This simple question implies how unfair Arthur has been. Their clash of viewpoints is seen in Arthur's response: '[*surprised*] Did you say "why?"?' His tone of voice and the repetition of the Inspector's question show that, to Arthur, placing one's own interests above those of others is the normal way to behave.

The Inspector suggests a different, more compassionate life based on empathy: 'it would do us all a bit of good if sometimes we tried to put ourselves in the place of these young women counting their pennies in their dingy little back bedrooms.'

How does this link to Eva Smith?

Eva represents the consequences of the survival of the fittest attitude.

Blaming the Birlings for putting their own lives above that of Eva, the Inspector describes his thoughts when viewing her dead body: 'A nice little promising life there, I thought, and a nasty mess somebody's made of it.'

Key Quotations to Learn

Arthur: '... a man has to make his own way ...' (Act 1)

Inspector (about Eva): 'But she died in misery and agony – hating life –' (Act 2)

Inspector: '... all intertwined with our lives, with what we think and say and do.' (Act 3)

Summary

- Arthur believes in survival of the fittest: looking after your own interests at the expense of others.
- The Inspector provides the opposite view: that members of society should look after each other.
- Eva Smith is used to represent the consequence of Arthur's viewpoint.

Sample Analysis

Arthur's belief in the survival of the fittest can be seen when he promotes his idea that 'a man has to mind his own business' to Eric and Gerald. This carries a double meaning, suggesting the importance of making money as well as the idea of ignoring the plight of others; the **auxiliary verb** shows that Birling sees this as vital to doing well in life. He continues with 'and look after himself and his own', which promotes selfishness as well as a sense, through the phrase 'his own', that poorer people are somehow different or below him. By repeating 'own', Priestley emphasises Birling's refusal to see himself as part of a wider society.

Questions

QUICK TEST
1. Who does Arthur encourage to follow self-interest?
2. What is symbolic about the arrival of the Inspector?
3. How does Eva represent the consequences of self-interest?
4. How are Arthur's words about self-interest reused by Eric in Act 3?

EXAM PRACTICE
Using one or more of the 'Key Quotations to Learn', write a paragraph analysing how Priestley presents Arthur's attitude of survival of the fittest.

Social Responsibility

You must be able to: analyse how social responsibility is explored in the play.

What is social responsibility?

Priestley uses the play to express his belief that we should help those people in society who are less fortunate than us. This is a key principle of socialism. He believes that capitalism focuses too much on individual gain.

How does Arthur Birling present a lack of social responsibility?

Arthur doesn't believe in social responsibility. His views are based on his capitalist ideals. He feels a responsibility to his family and his business, not to other people: 'it's my duty to keep labour costs down'.

He believes the poor are greedy and that the rich need to be careful and to not care about them or 'they'd soon be asking for the earth'. He thinks that for him to be wealthy and happy, others must be poor and unhappy.

How does Sybil Birling present a lack of social responsibility?

Despite being a prominent member of the Brumley Women's Charity Organisation, Sybil also lacks social responsibility. The charity helps young women who are 'deserving cases', suggesting the organisation is judgemental rather than compassionate.

She doesn't like Eva Smith and makes sure her case is refused. It is implied that she doesn't want to help because Eva is an unmarried mother, linking to the moral values of the time.

She refers to Eva as 'a girl of that sort' who was giving herself 'ridiculous airs'. This shows that she thinks working-class women are below her and should know their place.

How does the Inspector present social responsibility?

The Inspector is used by Priestley to promote social responsibility: 'their lives, their hopes and fears, their suffering, and chance of happiness, all intertwined with our lives, with what we think and say and do.'

The Inspector focuses on the vulnerable in society and how they need help: 'She needed not only money, but advice, sympathy, friendliness.'

When talking to Gerald and Sheila, he highlights his belief in social responsibility by including himself in the blame for Eva Smith's death: 'we'll have to share our guilt.'

He wants the Birlings to change: 'Remember what you did, Mrs Birling.'

Although the older members of the family don't seem to change, Sheila's and Eric's outlooks are altered by the Inspector.

Key Quotations to Learn

Arthur: '... like bees in a hive – community and all that nonsense.' (Act 1)

Inspector: '... it would do us all a bit of good if sometimes we tried to put ourselves in the place of these young women ...' (Act 1)

Inspector: 'You must have known what she was feeling. And you slammed the door in her face.' (Act 2)

Summary

- Priestley uses the Inspector to express the importance of social responsibility.
- He uses Arthur and Sybil Birling to represent how the higher classes focus on improving their own lives and status, rather than helping others.
- The Inspector changes Sheila's and Eric's social viewpoints but Arthur, Sybil and Gerald quickly return to their old selfishness.

Sample Analysis

Priestley uses the Inspector to explore social responsibility. In the comments he makes about society, 'We don't live alone. We are members of one body. We are responsible for each other', his **pattern of three** statements repeats the plural pronoun 'We' to emphasise socialist values of joint responsibility. The short sentences emphasise the messages that we should all respect and help each other, and this is captured in the **metaphor** 'one body'.

Questions

QUICK TEST
1. What does the Inspector believe we should do for the less fortunate people in society?
2. What is Arthur's opinion of social responsibility?
3. In what way does Sybil only pretend to have social responsibility?

EXAM PRACTICE
Using two or more of the 'Key Quotations to Learn', write a paragraph analysing how Priestley presents contrasting views about social responsibility.

Personal Responsibility

You must be able to: analyse how Priestley shows the different characters' attitudes to personal responsibility.

What is personal responsibility?

This means accepting the consequences of your own actions. As well as wanting the Birlings to understand why they should behave differently towards other people, the Inspector challenges each character to admit, and show guilt for, their individual role in Eva's suicide. In Act 3, Sheila refers to this as being made to 'confess'.

This is highlighted in one of the Inspector's final speeches: 'This girl killed herself – and died a horrible death. But each of you helped to kill her. Remember that. Never forget it.' The emotive language emphasises the effects of the characters' behaviour, while the two short imperative sentences focus on the necessity of accepting guilt.

Who accepts responsibility?

Sheila and Eric accept that they wronged Eva Smith.

In Act 3, Sheila says, 'I behaved badly too. I know I did. I'm ashamed of it.' Priestley emphasises her guilt through the repetition of the personal pronoun 'I' and uses short sentences that add a tone of certainty about her guilt.

The two children also point out the responsibility of the rest of the family, with Eric stating: 'the fact remains that I did what I did. And Mother did what she did. And the rest of you did what you did to her.' The use of **parallelism** at the end of each sentence emphasises the personal responsibility of everyone in the room, with the repetition of 'and' building up a sense of their negative impact on Eva's life.

Who doesn't accept responsibility?

While Gerald feels guilty in Act 2 for cheating on Sheila and for eventually deserting Eva, by the end of the play – because he thinks no one else knows – he seems to have forgotten his shame. He asks Sheila to remain engaged to him and doubts the story of Eva's death.

Throughout the play, Arthur claims that he was right to sack Eva Smith and justifies it using the word 'duty'. Sybil takes a similar point of view about refusing to help Eva, saying 'I had done no more than my duty.'

Priestley highlights Arthur and Sybil's lack of personal responsibility by also having them point out the failings of others. This is most obvious in the way Sybil, not realising she is criticising Eric, focuses on the responsibility of the man who made Eva pregnant, saying he should be made an example of and be forced to make a public confession.

Key Quotations to Learn

Summary

- The Inspector encourages each character to confess and take personal responsibility for the death of Eva Smith.
- Sheila and Eric accept responsibility.
- Gerald seems to show remorse but this fades when he thinks the story can be kept secret.
- Arthur and Sybil refuse to accept that they did anything wrong.

Sample Analysis

Priestley presents a lack of personal responsibility through Arthur's refusal to take any blame, 'There's every excuse for what both your mother and I did – it turned out unfortunately, that's all'. Including Sybil in the acknowledgment of his involvement shows his reluctance to accept any individual guilt. This is shown more clearly in the exaggerated noun phrase 'every excuse' to continue justifying his actions. The dramatic pause highlights the **callous** understatement of 'unfortunately', which combines with the dismissive phrase 'that's all' to suggest Arthur has no genuine sympathy for Eva's death.

Questions

QUICK TEST
1. Which characters take responsibility for their actions?
2. What word does Sheila use to describe the process of admitting what they did?
3. What do Arthur and Sybil do instead of taking responsibility?

EXAM PRACTICE
Using one or more of the 'Key Quotations to Learn', write a paragraph analysing how Priestley presents the theme of personal responsibility.

Inequality

You must be able to: analyse how Priestley shows the idea of inequality.

What is inequality?

Priestley's key socialist message is a response to the lack of equality in society. In the play, he explores how a lack of equality makes Eva Smith's life difficult and contributes to her death. Because the Birlings and Gerald have more money, status and power, their lives are much easier.

How does Eva represent inequality?

In terms of social **hierarchies**, Eva is at the bottom because she is working class and a woman. She always has people above her, controlling her life.

This can be seen in her working life, where she was easily fired from the factory and Milwards. It can also be seen in her personal life, forming relationships with Gerald and Eric where she is dependent on them financially and emotionally.

Because of her low status, Eva has a lack of opportunities. When Arthur asks what she did after being sacked, 'Get into trouble? Go on the streets?', crime and prostitution are presented as her most obvious options.

Her life is a struggle and references are made to her being penniless, hungry, lonely and preyed upon – sexually – by more powerful men.

How do the Birlings represent inequality?

In contrast to Eva, the Birlings represent power and fortune. They benefit from inequality.

The dining-room set and the meal they have just finished suggest wealth and an easy lifestyle.

Birling refers to their better opportunities when he mentions Eric's 'public-school-and-Varsity life'.

Their power comes from money but also their roles in society: Arthur is a magistrate, has been Lord Mayor, and is expecting a knighthood. In comparison, Eva would not even have had the vote (women didn't have the same voting rights as men until 1928).

As a wealthy client, Sheila has the power to have people sacked from Milwards. Similarly, Sybil has the power to influence who is helped by her charity.

How does the Inspector criticise inequality?

The Inspector criticises how working-class women are seen as 'cheap labour'.

As he investigates the family, he reveals the different ways they made Eva a victim of their social superiority.

He blames inequality for her suicide, saying her reason was 'Because she had been turned out and turned down too many times.' Priestley's use of the **passive voice** and repetition emphasise how Eva wasn't in control of her own life.

Key Quotations to Learn

Arthur: '... we're in for a time of steadily increasing prosperity.' (Act 1)

Sheila: 'But these girls aren't cheap labour – they're *people*.' (Act 1)

Gerald: '... she was desperately hard up ...' (Act 2)

Summary

- Eva Smith suffers from social inequality due to her class and her gender. There are always more powerful people controlling her life.
- Arthur and his family benefit from inequality as cheap labour has made them rich. Their abuse of power has led to Eva's death.

Sample Analysis

Priestley presents inequality by describing Eva's life after she is sacked, 'no work, no money coming in, ... no relatives to help her, few friends, lonely, half-starved, she was feeing desperate', and using a list to build up her struggle. The repetition of 'no' highlights aspects of Eva's social inequality. Placed after the Birlings' family celebration, the references to hunger and a lack of money and relatives create a contrast between Eva and the people who have ruined her life. The pattern of three adjectives at the end summarise the emotional and physical effects of this inequality.

Questions

QUICK TEST
1. Why is Eva socially unequal?
2. What things suggest the Birlings have greater power and opportunities?
3. How do the Birlings benefit from social inequality?

EXAM PRACTICE
Using one or more of the 'Key Quotations to Learn', write a paragraph analysing how Priestley presents the theme of inequality.

Young and Old

Video Solution / Exam Practice

You must be able to: analyse how Priestley explores the differences between youth and age.

How are traditional ideas about age shown in the play?

Traditionally, young people are expected to respect and obey their elders. These expectations were even more rigid at the start of the twentieth century.

When the play begins, Priestley gives Arthur the greatest number of lines to show he is in charge. He toasts the engagement, gives his opinions about the state of the world and goes on to lecture Eric and Gerald about life.

When he talks, he expects people to pay attention ('Are you listening, Sheila?'), doesn't like to be interrupted ('Just let me finish Eric') and gives opinions as facts ('The world's developing so fast it'll make war impossible').

Mrs Birling, although she lets her husband take the lead, also shows this dominance over the young, 'Please don't contradict me like that'.

Before the Inspector arrives, Eric and Sheila behave as tradition demands, for example, stopping squabbling when Sybil tells them off. Even when Eric tells his father not to make a speech, it is said '[not too rudely]' so the atmosphere on stage follows normal expectations.

Where are traditional age roles challenged?

When the Inspector arrives, Eric and Sheila begin to challenge the values of their parents. Both criticise Arthur's decision to sack Eva and, in Act 2, Sybil disapprovingly notes, 'You seem to have made a great impression on this child, Inspector.'

Sheila continues to challenge their behaviour, such as telling her father not to 'interfere' when he suggests she forgives Gerald or calling her mother's actions 'cruel and vile'. It is clear that she understands what the Inspector is doing whereas her parents do not.

Eric's response is more extreme. He curses his mother ('damn you'), is aggressive towards her ('[almost threatening her]') and mocks the **irony** of Arthur's after-dinner speech about self-interest.

How is Priestley using ideas about age?

By the end of the play, Eric and Sheila offer future hope. They represent the idea that society can change because they challenge their parents' refusal to alter their behaviour, with Sheila saying, 'You're ready to go on in the same old way. ... And it frightens me the way you talk.'

The Inspector's words have had a positive effect on them and they are beginning to develop a social conscience.

Key Quotations to Learn

Arthur: 'But you youngsters just remember what I said.' (Act 1)

Sheila (to Arthur): 'Oh – sorry. I didn't know. Mummy sent me in to ask you ...' (Act 1)

Eric: '[*shouting*] And I say the girl's dead and we all helped to kill her – and that's what matters – ' (Act 3)

Summary

- The young are expected to respect and obey their elders.
- At first, the Birlings display traditional expectations of age.
- After the Inspector's arrival, Sheila and Eric begin to challenge their parents.
- The children represent hope. Unlike their parents, they can learn and change.

Sample Analysis

Youth and age are explored through Arthur's response to Eric challenging his authority in Act 3: 'So hold your tongue if you want to stay here.' The **idiom** for being silent shows Arthur doesn't want his son to argue and its aggressive image represents his anger that traditional expectations of respect for ones' elders are being ignored. We know that Arthur is used to speaking and being listened to so Priestley's use of an imperative, and the threat of being made to leave home, suggests that Arthur is alarmed by the way he is being challenged by the younger generation.

Questions

QUICK TEST

1. What does Arthur show about the older generation at the start of the play?
2. What does Sheila show about the younger generation at the start of the play?
3. Why does Priestley make Sheila and Eric come into conflict with their parents?

EXAM PRACTICE

Using one or more of the 'Key Quotations to Learn', write a paragraph analysing how Priestley builds up conflict between the young and old.

You must be able to: analyse how Priestley uses ideas about time in the play.

How is the play linked to its time?

By setting the play several decades before he was writing, Priestley can use time to explore key ideas about its characters and themes.

In particular, Arthur's confidence in the *Titanic* and the impossibility of war creates dramatic irony that signals to the audience he isn't as wise as he thinks.

The Inspector's final words about 'fire and blood and anguish' refer to the two world wars that took place between the play's setting and when it was written. This allows the audience to reflect on the past and how and why society has changed.

How does Priestley use time to structure the play?

The play takes place over one evening with each act leading directly into the next, intensifying the destruction of the Birlings' cosy, self-centred way of life.

The series of **flashbacks** over a two-year period, as told by the characters, present Eva's life as a continual struggle against inequality. This emphasises the idea of a chain of events, consequences and the fact they cannot change the past.

By the end, the play has almost come full circle. Arthur, Sybil and Gerald are feeling safe and secure when they receive news that a police inspector is on his way. Priestley does this to convey the idea that, unless people change, society is doomed to keep making the same mistakes. He creates an intriguing cliffhanger ending that explores the idea of second chances; the audience are left wondering how the characters will respond to the consequences of their actions a second time around.

How does time affect the mood on stage?

The Inspector talks about needing to hurry in Act 3 and the quickened pace raises the tension on stage. It also adds to the story's mystery as the audience later realise the Inspector needed to finish before the real police arrived.

The play shows the past returning to haunt the characters. This allows Priestley to create a range of atmospheres on stage, such as Sheila's distress at how her previous actions have affected a woman's future, Gerald's desperation to keep his past secret, Sybil's shock at her son's past and Arthur's fear of future scandal.

While Eric and Sheila regret the past, Arthur and Sybil want to deny it. The Inspector says the characters will never forget what they did.

Key Quotations to Learn

Inspector: 'A chain of events ...' (Act 1)
Inspector (to Sybil): '... you're going to spend the rest of your life regretting it.' (Act 2)
Inspector: 'I haven't much time.' (Act 3)

Summary

- The short time-scale intensifies the events on stage.
- The flashbacks create an idea of past events and their consequences.
- Different responses to the past allow Priestley to create different moods on stage.
- Eric and Sheila want to mend the past while Arthur and Sybil deny it.

Sample Analysis

Priestley explores time through the idea that the past affects the present. For example,

Sybil: ... fine feelings and scruples that were simply absurd in a girl in her position.

Inspector: Her position now is that she lies with a burnt-out inside on a slab.

Priestley's **stichomythia** creates a chain of words which symbolises how Sybil's actions contributed to Eva's suicide. This is highlighted by the shift from her past tense to his present tense and the adverb 'now'. Sybil's mocking criticism of Eva, through the **alliterated** 'fine feelings' and the adjective 'absurd', is contrasted with the Inspector's brutal description to suggest she doesn't consider the consequences of her actions.

Questions

QUICK TEST
1. How is the past used to show the audience something about Arthur?
2. What is the effect of setting the play over one evening?
3. Why does Priestley use flashbacks in the play?
4. How do Sheila and Eric respond to the past differently to Arthur and Sybil?

EXAM PRACTICE
Using one or more of the 'Key Quotations to Learn', write a paragraph analysing how Priestley explores the theme of time in the play.

Love

You must be able to: analyse how Priestley presents the theme of love.

How is love presented at the start of the play?

The play opens with the family celebrating Sheila and Gerald's engagement. The stage directions show that Sheila should talk '[*gaily*]' and in a '[*playful*]' manner and this presents love in a happy way.

They seem deeply in love when they look at each other during the toast and Gerald says, 'And I drink to you – and hope I can make you as happy as you deserve to be.'

However, the audience might notice possible uncertainty in the **verb** 'hope' while the events of play bring some irony to the verb 'deserve'. Sheila's reaction to the ring ('Now I feel really engaged') could imply that money plays a role in their love. This returns when we realise Arthur's own reasons for approving of their engagement.

How are men and love presented?

Love is presented as meaning different things to men and women.

For Sheila and Eva, it represents faithfulness. When describing Eva's feelings for him, Gerald says, 'I became at once the most important person in her life', and the superlative suggests constancy and attachment.

Love is also linked to romance for women, with Sheila using fairy tale **imagery** to describe how Eva must have felt towards Gerald, 'You were the wonderful Fairy Prince.'

However, the men see love differently' with women being viewed as a commodity. Most obviously, Gerald has cheated on Sheila but expects her to resume their engagement at the end.

Gerald's and Eric's relationships are both linked to sex more than love. Gerald admits about Eva, 'I didn't feel about her as she felt about me', and the relationship is ended within six months.

In particular, Eric says of Eva, 'she was pretty and a good sport'. The use of the word 'sport' suggests that Eric sees love as a game rather than a serious commitment.

How are marriage and love presented?

Linking to the gender inequality of the time, it is suggested that the values of the young men are passed down by their parents.

Arthur tries to defend Gerald's behaviour to Sheila and it is suggested that his married friends have affairs.

Sybil points out that men focus more on business than marriage but says that Sheila will 'have to get used to that, just as I had.'

Key Quotations to Learn

Gerald (about Eva): 'She told me she'd been happier than she'd ever been before – but that she knew it couldn't last –' (Act 2)

Eric (about Eva): 'I wasn't in love with her or anything –' (Act 3)

Gerald: 'Everything's alright now, Sheila. [*Holds up the ring.*] What about this ring?' (Act 3)

Summary

- Priestley presents Gerald and Sheila as being in love.
- However, Gerald has had an affair.
- Men and women are presented as having different views of love.
- The men are criticised for wanting sex more than love.

Sample Analysis

There is a lack of honesty in Gerald's relationship with Sheila. In his reply to her question about Daisy Renton, 'All right. I knew her. Let's leave it at that', Gerald is hiding the truth from Sheila, particularly in the understatement of the second sentence. The short, **monosyllabic** sentences emphasise his reluctance to be honest with her. Rather than any apology, he ends with an imperative. This assertion of his male dominance, making a decision for 'us', links to attitudes of gender at the time. He thinks Sheila should not question his love but instead just accept whatever he says as the truth.

Questions

QUICK TEST
1. Where is marriage presented positively?
2. How does Sybil present a negative aspect of marriage?
3. What is different about men's and women's attitudes to love in the play?
4. How is Eric's relationship with Eva presented as being about sex?

EXAM PRACTICE
Using two or more of the 'Key Quotations to Learn', write a paragraph analysing how Priestley presents different attitudes to love.

Tips and Assessment Objectives

You must be able to: understand how to approach the exam question and meet the requirements of the mark scheme.

Quick tips

- You will get a choice of two questions. Do the one that best matches your knowledge, the quotations you have learned and the things you have revised.

- Make sure you know what the question is asking you. Underline key words and pay particular attention to the bullet point prompts that come with the question.

- You should spend about 45 minutes on your *An Inspector Calls* response. Allow yourself five minutes to plan your answer so there is some structure to your essay.

- Try to begin your essay with a clear statement, or thesis, that establishes your overall response to the exam question. This will give your essay a clearer focus and help you to explore the play as a whole.

- All your paragraphs should contain a clear idea, a relevant reference to the play (ideally a quotation) and analysis of how Priestley conveys this idea. Whenever possible, you should link your comments to the play's context.

- Keep your writing concise. If you waste time 'waffling' you won't be able to include the full range of analysis and understanding that the mark scheme requires.

- It is a good idea to remember what the mark scheme is asking of you.

AO1: Understand and respond to the play (12 marks)

This is all about coming up with a range of points that match the question, supporting your ideas with references from the play and writing your essay in a mature, academic style.

Lower	Middle	Upper
The essay has some good ideas that are mostly relevant. Some quotations and references are used to support the ideas.	A clear essay that always focuses on the exam question. Quotations and references support ideas effectively. The response refers to different points in the play.	A convincing, well-structured essay that answers the question fully. Quotations and references are well-chosen and integrated into sentences. The response covers the whole play (not everything, but ideas from all three acts rather than just focusing on one or two sections).

AO2: Analyse effects of Priestley's language, form and structure (12 marks)

You need to comment on how specific words, language techniques, sentence structures, stage directions or the narrative structure allow Priestley to get his ideas across to the audience. This could simply be something about a character or a larger idea he is exploring through the play. To achieve this, you will need to have learned good quotations to analyse.

Lower	Middle	Upper
Identification of some different methods used by Priestley to convey meaning. Some subject terminology.	Explanation of Priestley's different methods. Clear understanding of the effects of these methods. Accurate use of subject terminology.	Analysis of the full range of Priestley's methods. Thorough exploration of the effects of these methods. Accurate range of subject terminology.

AO3: Understand the relationship between the play and its contexts (6 marks)

For this part of the mark scheme, you need to show your understanding of how the characters or Priestley's ideas relate to when he was writing (1945) or when the play was set (1912).

Lower	Middle	Upper
Some awareness of how ideas in the play link to its context.	References to relevant aspects of context show a clear understanding.	Exploration is linked to specific aspects of the play's context to show a detailed understanding.

AO4: Written accuracy (4 marks)

You need to use accurate vocabulary, expression, punctuation and spelling. Although it's only four marks, this could make the difference between a lower or a higher grade.

Lower	Middle	Upper
Reasonable level of accuracy. Errors do not get in the way of the essay making sense.	Good level of accuracy. Vocabulary and sentences help to keep ideas clear.	Consistent high level of accuracy. Vocabulary and sentences are used to make ideas clear and precise.

Practice Questions

1. What do you think is the importance of the opening of *An Inspector Calls*?

   Write about:
   - How the opening of the play presents some important ideas
   - How Priestley presents these ideas by the ways he writes

2. How does Priestley use the character of Sybil to explore ideas about morality in *An Inspector Calls*?

   Write about:
   - How Priestley presents Sybil
   - How Priestley uses Sybil to explore some of his ideas

3. How does Priestley present some of the differences between social classes in *An Inspector Calls*?

   Write about:
   - How Priestley presents some of these differences
   - How Priestley explores differences between social classes in the play

4. 'In *An Inspector Calls*, Arthur Birling isn't used to being challenged'. Explore how far you agree with this statement.

   Write about:
   - How Priestley presents the character of Arthur
   - How Priestley uses the character of Arthur to explore some of his ideas

5. How does Priestley present attitudes towards responsibility in *An Inspector Calls*?

   Write about:
   - What some of the attitudes towards responsibility are
   - How Priestley presents some of these attitudes by the ways he writes

6. 'Eric is presented as the weakest character in *An Inspector Calls*'. Explore how far you agree with this statement.

   Write about:
   - How Priestley presents the character of Eric
   - How Priestley uses the character of Eric to explore some of his ideas

7. Who do you think shows the most regret for their actions in *An Inspector Calls*?

   Write about:
   - How Priestley presents your chosen character
   - How Priestley uses your chosen character to explore some of his ideas

8. How does Priestley present the Inspector as an unusual character in *An Inspector Calls*?

   Write about:
   - The ways the Inspector behaves and speaks to people
   - How Priestley presents the Inspector in the play

9. In *An Inspector Calls*, Sybil says 'I consider I did my duty'. How does Priestley explore attitudes towards duty?

   Write about:
   - How Priestley presents some of the attitudes towards duty
   - How Priestley uses these attitudes to explore ideas about society

10. How does Priestley present characters coming into conflict in *An Inspector Calls*?

Write about:

- Why some of the characters come into conflict
- How Priestley presents these characters coming into conflict

11. *An Inspector Calls* has been described as 'a play about inequality'. To what extent do you agree with this view?

Write about:

- How Priestley presents inequality
- How Priestley uses inequality to explore some of his ideas about society

12. How does Priestley present some of the differences between children and parents in *An Inspector Calls*?

Write about:

- How Priestley presents differences between children and parents
- How Priestley uses these differences to explore ideas about the generations in the play

13. At the start of *An Inspector Calls*, Arthur Birling tells Eric and Gerald: 'a man has to mind his own business and look after himself'.

How does Priestley present ideas about self-interest in the play?

Write about:

- What some of the ideas about self-interest are
- How Priestley presents these ideas by the ways he writes

14. How does Priestley present the relationship between Sheila and Gerald in *An Inspector Calls*?

Write about:

- What Sheila and Gerald's relationship is like
- How Priestley present their relationship by the ways he writes

15. How does Priestley use the Birlings to explore ideas about respectability in *An Inspector Calls*?

Write about:

- How Priestley presents ideas about respectability
- How Priestley uses the Birlings to explore some of his ideas

16. *An Inspector Calls* has been described as 'a play about secrets and lies'. To what extent do you agree with this view?

Write about:

- How Priestley presents secrets and lies
- How Priestley uses secrets and lies to explore some of his ideas about society

17. Are Mr and Mrs Birling 'good' parents?

Write about:

- How Priestley presents Arthur and Sybil as parents
- How Priestley uses Arthur and Sybil to explore ideas about being a parent

18. 'Sheila learns the most in *An Inspector Calls*.' Explore how far you agree with this statement.

Write about:

- How Priestley presents the character of Sheila
- How Priestley uses the character of Sheila to explore some of his ideas

Planning a Character Question Response

Video Solution · Exam Practice

You must be able to: understand what an exam question is asking you and prepare your response.

How might an exam question on character be phrased?

A typical character question will read like this:

> How and why does Eric change in *An Inspector Calls*? Write about:
> - How Eric responds to his family and to the Inspector
> - How Priestley presents Eric by the ways he writes   [30 marks + 4 AO4 marks]

How do I work out what to do?

The focus of this question is clear: Eric and how his character changes.

'How' and 'why' are important elements of this question.

For AO1, these words show that you need to display a clear understanding of what Eric is like, the ways in which he changes and the reasons for these changes.

For AO2, 'how' makes it clear that you need to analyse the different ways in which Priestley's use of language, structure and the dramatic form help to show the audience what Eric is like. Ideally, you should include quotations that you have learned but, if necessary, you can make a clear reference to a specific part of the play.

You also need to remember to link your comments to the play's context to achieve your AO3 marks and write accurately to pick up your four AO4 marks for spelling, punctuation and grammar.

How can I plan my essay?

You have approximately 45 minutes to write your essay.

This isn't long but you should spend the first five minutes writing a quick plan. This will help you to focus your thoughts and produce a well-structured essay.

Try to come up with a clear thesis statement that gives an overview of your response to the question, plus five or six linked ideas. Each of these ideas can then be written up as a paragraph.

You can plan in whatever way you find most useful. Some students like to just make a quick list of points and then re-number them into a logical order. Spider diagrams are particularly popular; look at the example on the opposite page.

In Act 1 seems childish – bickers with Sheila – later seems rather pleased when she's being questioned 'If you think that's the best she can do'

Questions his father's values (context of family/age in 1912) and shares similar feelings to Sheila by regretting his actions 'the fact remains that I did what I did'

How and why Eric changes

Dominated by his father (context of family in 1912) – gets cut off when trying to discuss the war and is patronised by him 'Yes, I know – but still – '

Reveals his feelings about his parents – they've never been there for him 'You don't understand anything. You never did. You never even tried – '

In Act 3, his true nature is revealed: he can get drunk and aggressive, has fathered a child out of wedlock (context of morality in 1912) and is a thief 'a chap easily turns nasty' '[*miserably*] I got it – from the office – '

Takes the opportunity to disagree with his father about the sacking of Eva Smith 'It isn't if you can't go and work somewhere else'

Summary

- Make sure you know what the focus of the essay is.
- Remember to analyse how ideas are conveyed by Priestley.
- Try to relate your ideas to the play's social and historical context.

Questions

QUICK TEST
1. What key skills do you need to show in your answer?
2. What are the benefits of quickly planning your essay?
3. Why is it better to have learned quotations for the exam?

EXAM PRACTICE
Plan a response to the follow exam question:
How and why does Sheila Birling change in *An Inspector Calls*? Write about:
- How Sheila responds to her family and to the Inspector
- How Priestley presents Sheila by the ways he writes   [30 marks + 4 AO4 marks]

Grade 5 Annotated Response

Video Solution   Exam Practice

How and why does Eric change in *An Inspector Calls*?

Write about:
- How Eric responds to his family and to the Inspector
- How Priestley presents Eric by the ways he writes

[30 marks + 4 AO4 marks]

Eric goes through some changes in 'An Inspector Calls'. He begins the play seeming spoiled and childish. He is a typical young man of his class. He laughs for no reason, squabbles with Sheila and enjoys trying to shock their mother (1). He is treated like a child by his parents, even though he's in his twenties. An example of this is when he tries to interrupt his father's speech to mention war but Arthur just cuts him off (2). The fact that he doesn't try to continue with his opinion shows that, as was expected of children at the time (3), he thinks he must respect his father.

However, Eric does begin to challenge his father more when the Inspector arrives. This could be because the Inspector doesn't show Arthur much respect (4). 'It isn't if you can't go and work somewhere else' (5). He says this to criticise his father's treatment of Eva Smith. 'Can't' and 'isn't' repeat the word 'not' to show he is contradicting his father's opinion (6). This also shows he has a better understanding of society than his father and this increasing wish to understand or care for others continues to the end of the play. 'The fact remains that I did what I did'. This shows that, unlike most of the family, Eric regrets what he did. The repetition of the phrase 'I did' shows he isn't trying to hide his guilt. He also agrees with his sister's fear of the Inspector's description of war. This shows that he now understands that the rich need to take more care of the poor and vulnerable in society.

The main reason Eric changes is because everyone finds out that he got Eva pregnant and stole money from the office and these actions would have been especially shocking when the play was first performed. Because of this he completely falls out with his parents. He says Arthur isn't 'the kind of father' that you can go to for help, which shows the audience his poor relationship with his father (7). When he realises that his mother could have helped Eva he says, 'Damn you'. This curse would have had more effect when the play was first performed as people were more religious (8). It shows he thinks his mother should go to hell for what she did and Arthur has to stop Eric from becoming more angry with Sybil, which is a big difference to the happy feeling at the start of the play when he's having a drink with his family (9).

The audience might also feel a bit sorry for Eric. He just seemed spoiled at the start. Now they can see he has a drinking problem. The Inspector lets him have a drink in Act 3 to help him 'get through'. This phrase shows that Eric is dependent on alcohol. However, he still treated Eva badly. The Inspector says Eric 'used' her and this verb shows that he just wanted her for sex (10). But by the end of the play he does seem a more serious person than before. He accepts the consequences of his actions, regrets what he did and refuses to laugh it all off, unlike Arthur, Sybil and Gerald (11).

1. The student makes an attempt to introduce the essay but it is vague instead of a specific thesis statement; the first paragraph has a clear idea and is supported by a reference to the play. AO1

2. There is some explanation of the methods Priestley uses to show Eric's character. This is limited by the lack of a quotation. AO2/AO1

3. Some historical context is used to explain Eric's behaviour but it is a little generalised. AO3

4. The new paragraph introduces a new point that is focused on the question of how and why Eric changes. AO1

5. A good quotation is used to support the idea. It would be better if it was embedded in a sentence. AO1

6. Clear analysis of the effects of Priestley's language choices. Some terminology is used. AO2

7. A quotation is embedded effectively but it isn't analysed. AO1/AO2

8. Context is used to develop the explanation of Priestley's language choices. AO3/AO2

9. The writing could be more careful and mature as the sentence is quite long and the vocabulary simple. However, the link back to the start of the play is an effective way of answering the exam question. AO1

10. A useful supporting quotation is embedded and then analysed, using terminology. AO1/AO2

11. The final paragraph offers some conclusion but is a little rushed. The essay could be structured more effectively as several ideas are included all at once. Writing is clear and accurate but doesn't enhance the essay. AO1/O4

Questions

EXAM PRACTICE
Choose a paragraph of this essay. Read it through a few times then try to rewrite and improve it. You might:
• improve the sophistication of the language or the clarity of expression
• replace a reference with a quotation or use a better quotation
• ensure quotations are embedded in the sentence
• provide more detailed, or a wider range of, analysis
• use more subject terminology
• link some context to the analysis more effectively.

Grade 7+ Annotated Response

A proportion of the best top-band answers will be awarded Grade 8 or Grade 9. To achieve this, you should aim for a sophisticated, fluid and nuanced response that displays flair and originality.

How and why does Eric change in *An Inspector Calls*? Write about:

• How Eric responds to his family and to the Inspector

• How Priestley presents Eric by the ways he writes   [30 marks + 4 AO4 marks]

Eric is initially presented as secretive and childish. However, once he is forced to admit his past bad behaviour, he begins to mature and understand the notion of responsibility (1).

At the start of the play, Eric's true nature is hidden from his family. Although Priestley includes him drinking on stage, the main impression we get is of a childish young man who bickers with his sister (2). When Sybil shows surprise at her daughter's use of the word 'squiffy', Eric adds sarcastically, 'If you think that's the best she can do – ' (3). He is clearly enjoying trying to shock their mother, who comes from a different generation and has different standards of etiquette (4).

*Eric's childishness is highlighted by how he is treated by his father (5). Arthur often patronises his son by referring to Eric's youth in contrast to his own experience. This is particularly apparent when Eric tries to give his opinion on the possibility of war. He begins, 'Yes, I know – but still – ' . However, just as he was by Sheila, he is cut off by his father and ignored. The pause between agreeing with his father and using the **conjunction** 'but' to open his contradiction shows he is nervous in front of Arthur (6).*

*Arthur's dominance over Eric is typical of father–son relationships, especially in the stricter early 1900s (7). However, when the Inspector begins questioning the family, we see Eric gain a bit more confidence and criticise his father's attitude towards the sacking of Eva, 'It isn't if you can't go and work somewhere else'. The two negative **verb phrases** show him contradicting not only his father's words but his father's right-wing social perspective (8).*

It is this move towards a more socialist view that is most dramatic in terms of how Eric changes (9). After the Inspector has gone, when the majority of the family are going back to their old behaviour, Eric accepts his responsibility: 'The fact remains that I did what I did.' His repetition underlines his guilt and, in turn, this also goes some way to repairing his relationship with his sister (10). When she refers to the Inspector's closing revolutionary image of 'Fire and blood and anguish', Eric agrees with its significance. He realises the need for the middle and upper classes to change their attitude to society's poor and vulnerable.

The turning point for Eric is the way in which his secret life is utterly exposed in front of his family by the Inspector (11). The audience find that this seemingly immature young man is an aggressive drunk who has stolen money from his own family and – of much greater immoral significance when the play was written and set than today – fathered a child out of wedlock. When he admits, 'a chap easily turns nasty', the adverb used could suggest he is making excuses that this is just how men behave but it actually shows his personal weaknesses. The adjective 'nasty' shows us the side that Eric has hidden from his family but Priestley's use of the impersonal noun phrase 'a chap' (instead of the personal pronoun I) allows this to characterise all of Eric's peers (12).

When he realises that his actions have led to Eva Smith's death, he accepts that he and his class are degenerate. This realisation breaks him but also signals the possible emergence of a better man (13).

1. A thesis statement establishes a clear overview of the student's approach to the question. AO1

2. The opening sentences establish a clear point about Eric. AO1

3. A relevant quotation is embedded as evidence. AO1

4. Eric's characterisation is linked to the social and historical context. AO3

5. The first point is developed further. AO1

6. Analysis of stagecraft, structure and language is used to show what Eric is like. AO2

7. Social context is used to link the previous point to the next point. AO1 and AO3

8. A relevant quotation and language analysis are used to show the first change in Eric. AO1 and AO2

9. Some evaluation is offered by making a judgement about Eric's biggest change of character. AO1 and AO2

10. Language analysis and social context are combined to show another change in Eric. AO2 and AO3

11. The reason for the change in Eric's character is examined. AO1

12. A variety of language analysis shows understanding of how Priestley conveys the reasons for Eric's change. AO2

13. The essay ends with a quick conclusive paragraph that, like the rest of the essay, is well-written and contains some precise, sophisticated language. AO1 and AO4

Questions

EXAM PRACTICE

Spend 45 minutes writing an answer to the following question:

How and why does Sheila Birling change in *An Inspector Calls*? Write about:

• How Sheila responds to her family and to the Inspector

• How Priestley presents Sheila by the ways he writes

[30 marks + 4 AO4 marks]

Remember to use the plan you have already prepared.

Planning a Theme Question Response

You must be able to: understand what an exam question is asking you and prepare your response.

How might an exam question on theme be phrased?

A typical theme question will read like this:

How does Priestley present attitudes towards the working classes in *An Inspector Calls*? Write about:

• What some of the attitudes towards the working classes are

• How Priestley presents some of these attitudes by the ways he writes

[30 marks + 4 AO4 marks]

How do I work out what to do?

The focus of this question is clear: attitudes towards the working classes.

'What' and 'how' are important elements of this question.

For AO1, 'what' shows that you need to display a clear understanding of the different attitudes characters have.

For AO2, 'how' makes it clear that you need to analyse the different ways in which Priestley's use of language, structure and the dramatic form help to show these attitudes. Ideally, you should include quotations that you have learned but, if necessary, you can make a clear reference to a specific part of the play.

You also need to remember to link your comments to the play's context to achieve your AO3 marks and write accurately to pick up your four AO4 marks for spelling, punctuation and grammar.

How can I plan my essay?

You have approximately 45 minutes to write your essay.

This isn't long but you should spend the first five minutes writing a quick plan. This will help you to focus your thoughts and produce a well-structured essay.

Try to come up with a clear thesis statement that gives an overview of your response to the question, plus five or six linked ideas. Each of these ideas can then be written up as a paragraph.

You can plan in whatever way you find most useful. Some students like to just make a quick list of points and then re-number them into a logical order. Spider diagrams are particularly popular; look at the example on the opposite page.

Arthur and Gerald see nothing wrong in exploiting them
'it's my duty to keep labour costs down'
(Context: Capitalism vs Socialism)

Arthur and Gerald feel that they need to be kept in their place
'If you don't come down sharply on some of these people, they'd soon be asking for the earth'
(Context: national strike 1912)

The Inspector warns that the working classes will rise up
'they will be taught it in fire and blood and anguish'

Attitudes towards the working classes

Sheila and Eric agree that the middle class needs to change its attitude towards the working class
'So there's nothing to be sorry for, nothing to learn. We can all go on behaving just as we did'

The Inspector feels that the working class need to be treated better
'We don't live alone. We are members of one body. We are responsible for each other'
(Context: rise of trade unions/Labour Party)

Sybil thinks the working class are naturally less respectable than her
'As if a girl of that sort would ever refuse money!'

Summary

- Make sure you know what the focus of the essay is.
- Remember to analyse how ideas are conveyed by Priestley.
- Try to relate your ideas to the play's social and historical context.

Questions

QUICK TEST
1. What key skills do you need to show in your answer?
2. What are the benefits of quickly planning your essay?
3. Why is it better to have learned quotations for the exam?

EXAM PRACTICE
Plan a response to the follow exam question:
How does Priestley present attitudes towards guilt in *An Inspector Calls*? Write about:
• What some of the attitudes towards guilt are
• How Priestley presents some of these attitudes by the ways he writes
[30 marks + 4 AO4 marks]

Grade 5 Annotated Response

Video Solution | Exam Practice

How does Priestley present attitudes towards the working classes in *An Inspector Calls*? Write about:

• What some of the attitudes towards the working classes are

• How Priestley presents some of these attitudes by the ways he writes

[30 marks + 4 AO4 marks]

In Act 1, Arthur shows that he doesn't care about the working classes (1). 'It's my duty to keep labour costs down' (2). He sees them as a workforce rather than as individuals with their own lives and problems. Because he uses the word 'duty' it shows he thinks his view is morally correct (3). This links to the way in which he sacked Eva for going on strike because he doesn't think she has the right to ask for more money (and probably doesn't understand why she needs more money).

Arthur and Gerald both believe that the working classes need to be treated harshly. This is shown when they both agree about Arthur's treatment of Eva Smith 'asking for the earth'. This shows that they think the working classes could take over because it uses a big image 'earth'. This links to the strikes that were going on at the time the play is set (4). It also shows (5) that they want to make as much money as possible for themselves rather than share it out.

Sheila and Eric change their views about the working classes. At first they seem very selfish but when they realise what they have done to Eva Smith they change (6). Sheila believes that the family (and the rest of society) need to behave in a more caring way so when the others go back to normal at the end she sarcastically says, 'So there's nothing to be sorry for, nothing to learn. We can all go on behaving just as we did'. (7) She repeats the word 'nothing' in order to criticise the other characters. The verbs she uses ('to be sorry' and 'learn') show how Eva's story has affected her (8). She feels guilty and has a different attitude to the one she had when she got Eva sacked from Milwards.

In contrast to Arthur and Gerald (9), the Inspector has a compassionate attitude towards the working classes. He thinks that they need to be cared for and uses Eva Smith as an example of this throughout the play. He argues with Arthur about him sacking Eva Smith and criticises how the cities and towns are full of poor people being exploited by factories like Birlings and Crofts. At the end of the play, he tells he characters, 'We don't live alone. We are members of one body. We are responsible for each other.' The word 'we' is repeated three times to emphasise the idea that everyone should look after each other rather than being separate and this is highlighted in the image of 'one body' to show how society needs to function together. This was also Priestley's view as he was a socialist like his father (10).

Sybil shares the views of Arthur and Gerald because she is old-fashioned. She describes Eva Smith as 'a girl of that sort'. This phrase shows that she looks down on the working classes. She thinks she *is morally superior to them as they are poor and get pregnant out of wedlock. Priestley makes her attitude hypocritical because she runs a charity but isn't actually charitable. She only does it to make herself look good (11).*

1. The essay would benefit from starting with a clear thesis statement; the opening sentence establishes a clear point about attitudes towards the working class. AO1
2. A relevant quotation is used as evidence but it would be better if it was embedded. AO1
3. Explanation of how Priestley conveys meaning with some analysis of language. AO2
4. Context included. It is linked to the explanation but in quite a general way. AO3
5. The essay is clearly written but the language isn't sophisticated. The same phrase is used several times in this paragraph. AO4
6. Mentioning how characters change shows understanding of the play as a whole. AO1
7. Relevant quotation, partially embedded in the sentence. AO1
8. Some detailed analysis of the effects of language. AO2
9. A new paragraph is used for a new point and there are a range of ideas. However, the essay could be better structured as the opening sentence links to the paragraph before the previous one. AO1
10. Some detailed analysis linked to context. More subject terminology could be used. AO2/AO3
11. The final paragraph shows good understanding but would benefit from being shaped into a clearer conclusion. AO1/AO2

Questions

EXAM PRACTICE
Choose a paragraph of this essay. Read it through a few times then try to rewrite and improve it. You might:
• Improve the sophistication of the language or the clarity of expression.
• Replace a reference with a quotation or use a better quotation.
• Ensure quotations are embedded in the sentence.
• Provide more detailed, or a wider range of, analysis.
• Use more subject terminology.
• Link some context to the analysis more effectively.

A proportion of the best top-band answers will be awarded Grade 8 or Grade 9. To achieve this, you should aim for a sophisticated, fluid and nuanced response that displays flair and originality.

How does Priestley present attitudes towards the working classes in *An Inspector Calls*? Write about:

• What some of the attitudes towards the working classes are

• How Priestley presents some of these attitudes by the ways he writes

[30 marks + 4 AO4 marks]

Priestley presents contrasting attitudes towards the working classes. While the Birling family illustrate old-fashioned, discriminatory values, he uses the Inspector to encourage a more modern, socialist viewpoint (1).

In Act 1, Priestley uses Arthur and Gerald to represent the traditional middle-class attitude that the working class are there to be exploited and need to be kept in their place (2). When Arthur says, 'it's my duty to keep labour costs down' (3), the lack of personalisation in the noun phrase 'labour costs' suggests the working classes are not valued individuals but just a resource to be used. The word 'costs' also implies that they are a source of annoyance, as if he shouldn't have to pay them at all. Priestley has Arthur use the **abstract noun** *'duty' to show he feels his attitude is justified as it is based on solidarity with his fellow businessmen (4).*

When he argues that, 'If you don't come down sharply on these people, they'd soon be asking for the earth', Priestley shows Arthur's distrust for the working class with the adverb 'sharply' implying they should be treated harshly, even violently. Linking to the labour strikes of 1912, Birling fears they will take what he thinks rightfully belongs to the middle class (5). Priestley employs **hyperbole** *in the metaphor 'asking for the earth' to show how ridiculous Arthur's view is but has Gerald agree to show it isn't just an isolated attitude (6).*

Similarly, Sybil displays snobbery towards the working classes in Act 2, saying of Eva, 'as if a girl of that sort would ever refuse money!' The dismissive phrase 'that sort' shows that Sybil has no respect for the working class. The phrase 'as if' and the exclamation mark suggest this line should be said in a mocking tone (7). Rather than being sympathetic towards their poverty, she sees it as their moral failure. Priestley does this to point out the hypocrisy of the church-based charities (like the one Sybil chairs) that claimed to help the poor but actually sat in judgement on them.

Through the Inspector, Priestley challenges these attitudes and offers an alternative view that the working class need to be treated better (8). When the Inspector says, in Act 3, 'We don't live alone. We are members of one body. We are responsible for each other', Priestley uses rhetorical techniques to increase the impact of the speech. The pattern of three short sentences emphasises the need for society to unite and look after its less fortunate groups (9). This idea of unity is then highlighted by the repetition of the plural pronoun 'we' and reflects the socialist views that were gathering popularity in the early twentieth century (10).

Sheila and Eric represent hope for the future because their attitude towards the working class changes to one of compassion. At the end, Priestley gives Sheila a tone of irony when she says, 'So there's nothing to be sorry for, nothing to learn. We can all go on behaving just as we did.' The different verb phrases focus on the need to accept that the middle-class attitude to the working class has been wrong and that they need to learn from their mistakes and change.

The play establishes traditional attitudes towards the working classes, uses the story of Eva Smith to show their damaging consequences and then offers a better alternative (11). First performed after the Second World War, the Inspector's emotive reference to 'fire and blood and anguish' reminds the audience of the role the working classes played in maintaining the wealth and freedom of the rest of society, thereby highlighting the rightfulness of social equality to the audience not just to the characters on stage (12).

1. A thesis statement establishes a clear overview of the student's approach to the question. AO1
2. The opening sentence establishes a clear point about attitudes towards the working class. AO1
3. A relevant quotation is embedded as evidence. AO1
4. Priestley's use of language to convey meaning is analysed in detail. AO2
5. Specific context is used to enhance the analysis. AO3
6. Detailed analysis includes a range of subject terminology. AO2
7. Analysis includes approaching the play as a performance. AO2
8. A new paragraph changes the focus of this well-structured essay. AO1
9. Analysis of the effects of sentence structure. AO2
10. Analysis of language is enhanced by contextual links. AO2/AO3
11. The essay ends with a well-structured conclusion. There is a sense of the play as a whole, reinforced during the essay by quotations from across the three acts. AO1
12. Analysis is linked to the play as a performance and to context. AO2/AO3

Questions

EXAM PRACTICE
Spend 45 minutes writing an answer to the following question:
How does Priestley present attitudes towards guilt in *An Inspector Calls*? Write about:
• What some of the attitudes towards guilt are
• How Priestley presents some of these attitudes by the ways he writes
[30 marks + 4 AO4 marks]
Remember to use the plan you have already prepared.

Glossary

Abstract noun – a noun that is an idea or quality rather than a concrete object (such as: charity, compassion).

Adjective – a word that gives more information about a noun.

Adverb – a word that gives more information about a verb.

Alliteration – a series of words beginning with the same sound.

Atmosphere – the mood or emotion in a play.

Auxiliary verb – a verb used to show the tense of another verb (such as: *are* eating, *were* eating).

Callous – uncaring and cruel.

Capitalist – a right-wing political belief in individual gain, through hard work and a focus on profit.

Cliffhanger – ending an act with a shock or problem.

Climax – the most intense part of an act or the whole play.

Colloquialism – everyday, slang word.

Compassion – sympathetic concern.

Confession – a statement admitting guilt; (in religion) acknowledging sin.

Conflict – a disagreement or argument.

Conjunction – a word that links words, phrases and clauses together in a sentence (such as: and, but, while).

Conscience – a person's sense of right and wrong.

Convention – an expected way in which something is usually done.

Depression (economic) – when less spending causes businesses to close and unemployment to rise, leading to even less spending.

Determiner – a word that shows whether a reference is specific (such as: this, that, your, his) or general (such as: a, an, any).

Dominance – having power and influence over others.

Dramatic irony – when the audience of a play is aware of something that a character on stage isn't.

Dramatic pause – a pause in speech to create a specific effect on stage.

Emotive – creating or describing strong emotions.

Etiquette – a code of polite behaviour in society.

Exploited – used in an unfair way (for the user's benefit).

Flashback – a dramatic device taking a play back in time.

Foreshadow – hint at future events in the play.

Hierarchy – a ranking according to status and power.

Hoax – a humorous or nasty trick.

Hyperbole – exaggeration to emphasise an idea.

Hypocrisy – claiming to have better standards or behaviour than is true.

Idiom – a colloquial phrase with figurative, rather than literal, meaning.

Illegitimate – a person whose parents aren't married.

Imagery – words used to create a picture in the imagination.

Imperative sentence – an sentence that gives an order.

Industrial Revolution – a period when machinery started to be used much more in production, leading to big factories rather than small businesses.

Inferior – being less important than others.

Interrogative – a question.

Irony – something that seems the opposite of what was expected; deliberately using words that mean the opposite of what is intended.

Justified – something done for a good, fair reason.

Juxtapose – place two contrasting things side by side.

Metaphor – a descriptive technique, using comparison to say one thing is something else.

Modal verb – a verb that shows the necessity or possibility of another verb (such as: *could* eat, *should* eat, *might* eat).

Monosyllabic – words containing only one syllable.

Noun – a naming word for a person, place, animal or object.

Noun phrase – a group of words that functions like a noun.

Objective – not influenced by personal feelings or opinions.

Omniscient – all-knowing.

Parallelism – repeating similar word orders or sentence constructions to emphasise an idea.

Passive voice – where the subject of a sentence has something done to it (in contrast to active voice, where the subject of the sentence does something).

Patriarch – the male head of a family.

Patronising – talking in a nice way that actually implies a belief in the superiority of the speaker.

Pattern of three – three related ideas, placed together for emphasis.

Prejudiced – being against someone because of an already-formed idea, rather than fact or experience.

Pronoun – a word that takes the place of a noun (such as: I, she, them, it).

Provincial – living beyond a major city, suggesting a lack of sophistication.

Respectable – seen as good and proper by society.

Retrospect – looking back on the past with the benefit of current knowledge.

Rhetorical question – a question asked in order to create thought rather than to get a specific answer.

Simile – a descriptive technique, using comparison to say one thing is 'like' or 'as' something else.

Sin – an immoral act.

Stichomythia – lines in a play alternating between two characters but repeating certain words to emphasise specific ideas.

Strike – when workers refuse to work as a form of protest.

Suburb – a (usually quite well-off) residential area on the outskirts of a town or city.

Superior – being better or more important than others.

Superlative – the most something can be (for example: biggest, highest, coldest).

Symbolise – when an object or colour represents a specific idea or meaning.

Taboo – a word or action that is not allowed, or looked down on, due to social expectations.

Tense – the changing of words or word endings to show when things are taking place (past, present, future).

Tension – a feeling of anticipation, discomfort, or excitement in a play.

Traditional – long-established or old-fashioned.

Verb – a word that expresses an action or state of being.

Verb phrase – a group of words containing at least one verb and its dependents – objects, complements and other modifiers.

Welfare state – a system in which the government looks after the poor and vulnerable in society.

Womanising – having various casual affairs with women.

Answers

Pages 4–5

Quick Test

1. Arthur and Sybil, and their children, Eric and Sheila.
2. Sheila's engagement to Gerald Croft.
3. To investigate the suicide of a young woman, Eva Smith.
4. Eva worked at Arthur's factory and was sacked after helping to organise a strike in demand of higher wages.
5. Arthur thinks the sacking was justified and Gerald agrees. Eric and the Inspector show sympathy for Eva's situation.

Exam Practice

Answers might consider how the mood is conveyed by Arthur's happiness and/or Gerald's cheerful behaviour and praise.

Analysis might include the effect of the superlative adjective 'happiest' and/or the noun phrase 'nice well-behaved family'. The stage direction '[*laughs*]' could also be used to explain how the men's relaxed behaviour creates a happy and contented mood.

Pages 6–7

Quick Test

1. Sheila feels sorry for Eva.
2. She thought Eva was laughing at her. She was in a bad mood and jealous of her looks.
3. She's upset about Eva, which shows some guilt, but she's also upset for herself and how her evening has been spoiled, which highlights the selfish side of her character.
4. Gerald.
5. She was having an affair with Gerald.

Exam Practice

Answers might focus on Sheila changing her attitude towards the Inspector and accepting her guilt, or Gerald wanting to keep his secrets from the Inspector.

Analysis might include Sheila's tone of voice in the stage direction, her use of questions, Gerald's imperative or his slightly **taboo** language.

Pages 8–9

Quick Test

1. To hide his involvement from the Inspector and to hide further details from Sheila.
2. She refers to her lower-class status.
3. She acts in a grand and superior manner.
4. Sybil is behaving how the others behaved before the Inspector exposed them.
5. It started as him innocently helping her but then they became lovers.

Exam Practice

Answers might explore the Inspector and Gerald's sympathy for her or Sybil's snobbery.

Analysis might include the Inspector's use of the plural pronoun 'we' and use of the abstract noun 'guilt', Gerald's adjective 'little' to show Eva's small needs or Sybil's **determiner** 'that' to emphasise her disgust of the lower classes.

Pages 10–11

Quick Test

1. She was using the false name Mrs Birling.
2. No, she thinks it was justified.
3. Sheila thinks it was horrible; Arthur worries it might make them look bad.
4. She thought Eva was lying about the lover offering money but her refusing because she thought it was stolen.
5. Sheila works out that Eric was the father of Eva's child before her parents do.

Exam Practice

Answers will centre on Sybil's lack of compassion for Eva and her refusal to see that she treated her badly.

Analysis might focus on the insincerity of the apology (due to the 'But' that begins the next sentence and her placing of blame), her prejudice of Eva based on her class, this dismissive phrase 'that sort', the exclamation mark suggesting mockery of Eva or her harshness causing Sheila's urgent response.

Pages 12–13

Quick Test

1. He gets drunk and aggressive.
2. She knew he didn't love her.
3. Murdering Eva along with her own grandchild.
4. He wants to cover up the evening's revelations.
5. That we are all responsible for each other in society and change must come.

Exam Practice

Answers might focus on Arthur's lack of social responsibility, his temper or his failures as a parent.

Analysis might include his tone of voice in the stage direction, Eric's negative image of Arthur or the Inspector's criticism of Arthur's attitudes through his pattern of three short sentences all beginning with the plural pronoun 'we'.

Pages 14–15

Quick Test

1. They want to avoid any scandal.
2. Their sense of responsibility for Eva's death.
3. Relieved with a sense that things can go back to normal. They make a joke of it all.
4. They still know that, individually, they ruined a woman's life.
5. A phone call reveals that a woman has been found dead and an inspector is coming to interview them.

Exam Practice

Answers will explore the children's guilt in contrast with their parents' refusal to accept responsibility and instead forget the evening's events.

Analysis might include Sheila's repetition of 'had happened' emphasised by the adverb 'really', her short sentences emphasise how her parents haven't changed, Arthur's exclamation and cheerful stage directions, the future **tense** to show his confidence or his jovial language conflicting with Sheila's serious language.

Pages 16–17

Quick Test

1. There's only one set, the play takes place (without changes in time between the Acts) over one evening and characters are generally focused on one at a time.
2. Use of cliffhangers to raise tension.
3. Character confessions lower the tension whilst family conflict raises it.
4. His social message about having personal and social responsibility.

Exam Practice

Analysis might include Sheila's fear of the Inspector's knowledge and the repeated short sentences in the future tense to create a sense of warning, Arthur's shock shown through his short exclamation and his tone of voice along with the dramatic pauses signalled by the dashes, the final stage direction creating a cliffhanger through silence and facial expressions.

Pages 18–19

Quick Test

1. The Crofts.
2. The Birlings.
3. Working class.
4. Capitalist. He is a business man and focuses on making money.

Exam Practice

Comments might include how the pause before Lady Croft's name, the use of her title and the defence of her snobbery shows Arthur's respect for the upper classes and his wish to be like them. As a capitalist, he believes in the importance of money and status. We also know, from Act 1, that he hopes a marriage between the Crofts and the Birlings will help to improve his business and his social position. He points out that the Crofts are from an old, land-owning family, reminding us that Birling represents the new wealth of the middle classes benefitting from the Industrial Revolution. He boasts about the possibility of the Honours List and a knighthood, showing that he sees a title as a way to become equal in status if not breeding.

Pages 20–21

Quick Test

1. The Inspector represents Priestley's socialist views about looking after everyone in society.
2. Fighting alongside men of all different classes may have influenced Priestley's belief in equality.
3. They established the welfare state, the National Health Service and new housing plans where people of different classes would live side by side.

Exam Practice

Arthur's noun phrase 'steadily increasing prosperity' would seem ironic given the economic depression that followed the First World War. The capitalist comments would also have conflicted with the growth of trade unions and the popularity of socialism after the Second World War, signalled by the Labour Party's landslide election win in 1945.

Pages 22–23

Quick Test

1. There was no social security or free health care.
2. Home, workplace, church and government.
3. Women were seen as unequal to men and were expected to stay at home and bring up a family, they had less access to jobs and promotion and had fewer legal rights.

Exam Practice

Comments might include: how Arthur's tone of voice and **rhetorical question** show that he is critical of sex outside of marriage, which links to Christian values; Eric's ironic adjective 'respectable' when discussing Arthur's friends who have affairs suggests the double standards of the middle classes, often ignoring their own immoral behaviour to focus on criticising others; how this is emphasised when Arthur interrupts Eric to keep him quiet; the implication that women are less moral (and less important) than men.

Pages 24–25

Quick Test

1. The furniture, the glasses, the cigar box.
2. It isn't very cosy or homely.
3. The lighting is warm, the props suggest quality or luxury and the characters are sitting down.
4. The lighting becomes brighter and harder when the Inspector arrives, to emphasise that they are being interrogated and exposed.

Exam Practice

Comments might focus on the look of the furniture and how it suggests both wealth and self-confidence, the size of the room and the expensive props such as champagne glasses or how the wealthy characters are seated whilst the maid clears up after them.

Pages 26–27

Quick Test

1. People in society should care for each other.
2. He doesn't show respect for the Birlings' higher status.
3. Goole/ghoul suggests mystery and perhaps the idea that the Inspector isn't 'real'.
4. He reveals their secrets and their bad behaviour, challenging their view of themselves.

Exam Practice

Answers might explore the Inspector's social morality or his wish to see justice done.

Analysis could include the list of contrasts that show that people should care about the struggles of the working classes, the rhetorical question and abstract noun 'duty' to suggest his moral crusade or the short sentences with their negative images to show the consequences of a lack of social morality.

Pages 28–29

Quick Test

1. To establish his dominant character and his status as the head of the family.
2. 'hard-headed business man'
3. He hopes it will link his factory with Croft's factory and improve his social status.
4. Because we know there was a war two years later, it shows he isn't as clever as he thinks and doesn't really understand society/the world.

Exam Practice

Analysis might focus on his patronising tone of voice to Gerald and Eric, his regular use of the conjunction 'and' to show he thinks he has a lot to tell people, the adjectives he applies boastfully to himself, the contrast between 'guess'/'know' to criticise others and make himself sound wiser, the emphasis on 'know' and the use of pauses around 'experience' to show his self-belief or his use of the plural pronoun 'we' to place him alongside other hardworking, clever businessmen.

Pages 30–31

Quick Test

1. She usually takes Arthur's lead and follows his instructions.
2. Because she believes she lives a moral life and she thinks her wealth and social status make her more important. She draws on Arthur's status to support this.
3. She's a hypocrite. She pretends to care but just likes to judge.
4. She treats him like a child, doesn't understand his feelings and is unaware of his problems.

Answers

Exam Practice

Answers might focus on her disregard for Eva Smith or her unwillingness to see what Eric is really like.

Analysis could comment on the rude use of the determiner 'that', her placing of blame and the rigid adverb 'only', her statements to Eric that are about him and are all wrong, her comment about Eric not getting drunk that contrasts with his behaviour in Act 1 and what she's told by Sybil and Gerald in Act 2.

Pages 32–33

Quick Test

1. She is the daughter of a wealthy businessman and is dating a man from an upper-class family.
2. She thinks she is being laughed at, is in a bad mood and is jealous of Eva's prettiness.
3. She begins to accept her responsibility and sympathise with Eva's life.
4. Sheila realises that Eric was the father of Eva's child.

Exam Practice

Answers could explore how she changes or she sees how the family are making matters worse for themselves.

Analysis might include her repetition of 'never', the hanging metaphor and the dramatic pause before it to link to them making their crimes (and the possible punishment) worse or her repetition of the verb 'begged' to show she knew better than her mother what the Inspector was doing.

Pages 34–35

Quick Test

1. He isn't paired with another character (like Arthur/Sybil and Sheila/Gerald) so seems isolated, he is the last to speak and he behaves strangely.
2. He thinks they had every right to go on strike and his father treated them badly.
3. He is ashamed.
4. He dislikes them and feels they've never tried to understand him.

Exam Practice

Analysis might include the use of the **interrogative** 'why' to challenge his father's decisions, the use of language that would shock his parents, his ironic use of the adjective 'respectable' to criticise his father's peers or his **emotive** accusation against his mother followed by the repeated cursing.

Pages 36–37

Quick Test

1. He refers to himself as 'respectable' and has hidden his affair from his fiancée.
2. Arthur appreciates Gerald as a businessman but is more interested in his social status as a member of the upper classes.
3. He gave her food and found her somewhere to live.
4. He started an affair with her and then broke her heart.

Exam Practice

Analysis might include how the contrasting noun and noun phrase show that he tries to hide his personal crimes, the **modal verb** 'can' showing he thinks he can deceive the Inspector and the plural pronoun 'we' encouraging Sheila to help him despite his affair or the two short sentences contrasting past and present tense to show his acceptance that he has done something wrong.

Pages 38–39

Quick Test

1. The working class and women.
2. Arthur sacks her for wanting more money, Sheila has her sacked unfairly, Gerald helps her but then makes her his lover and breaks her heart, Eric gets her pregnant and Sybil refuses to help her.
3. She is hardworking (as opposed to Sheila and Eric) and she refuses to take Eric's money once she thinks it is stolen.
4. Edna's role as a servant shows that the Birlings are happy to employ people to fulfil their needs; the idea of having someone below them, in a position of inequality, does not trouble them.

Exam Practice

Analysis might focus on how numbers ('a lot'/'every') show that Eva represents all working-class women, the list of adjectives to describe a typical life of suffering or the verb 'used' and the dehumanising descriptions to show how the working class aren't valued by those above them. The third quotation also explores the idea that the working classes are defined by others (mostly, but not exclusively, men), with Eva's story only heard through others.

Pages 40–41

Quick Test

1. Public scandal.
2. Eric and Sheila accept their guilt and know they need to change; their parents refuse to accept any responsibility.
3. He asks her to take the engagement ring again.
4. Their lack of closeness and understanding has now been exposed and their relationship has deteriorated.

Exam Practice

Analysis might consider: Arthur's mention of 'public scandal' alongside the repetition of the future tense 'will' so show his fears, the use of 'I' and 'we' (meaning the family) to show his self-interest and the exaggerated verb 'suffer' to show his concern for himself not Eva, showing that he hasn't changed; Sybil now finding the evening amusing, implying no change in her outlook; Sheila's accusation that shows she has learned but her family have not; or Eric's use of the verb 'pretend' to show how he now sees the Birlings' respectability is all an act.

Page 42–43

Quick Test

1. His wish for more money and status.
2. He used Eva for sexual gratification and he drinks too much.
3. Eva's prettiness.
4. When she refers to her status or her belief that she has the right to judge others.

Exam Practice

Analysis might include the Inspector's use of the word 'jealous' to link this sin to Sheila, Sybil's noun phrase 'gross impertinence' to show that she was superior to Eva, her pride in her family name (and not knowing that Eva has some claim to the name) and Eric's admission that he didn't love Eva which includes the phrase 'or anything' to emphasise how shallow his feelings were.